*The*
# POWER
*of*
# INFLUENCE


**Yoritomo-Tashi** was the founder of the first Japanese dynasty of Shoguns, and one of the greatest statemen Japan has ever had. He was also a well-known philosopher who was admired by his people. He wrote extensively on philosophical subjects, which are encapsulated in books such as *Common Sense: How to Exercise It* and *The Power of Influence*.

*The*

# POWER

*of*

# INFLUENCE

*Timeless Strategies, Modern Triumph*
The Statesman's Guide to *Mastering Life*

RUPA

Published by
Rupa Publications India Pvt. Ltd 2024
7/16, Ansari Road, Daryaganj
New Delhi 110002

*Sales centres:*
Bengaluru Chennai
Hyderabad Jaipur Kathmandu
Kolkata Mumbai Prayagraj

P-ISBN: 978-93-6156-681-3
E-ISBN: 978-93-6156-382-9

First impression 2024

10 9 8 7 6 5 4 3 2 1

Printed in India

# CONTENTS

# 1

# BY THE INCREASE AND SPREAD
# OF PSYCHIC FORCES

"There is a country situated no far from the River Yet-Sin," said Yoritomo, "wherein certain villages are renowned for the curative property of the air."

"With the lightest breezes are diffused balsamic odours, which pour into weak lungs the restoring breath they pant for. At the coming of spring invalids gather there to install themselves temporarily in tiny houses which, seen from a distance, look like huge birds resting for an instant before retaking flight."

"My venerated master, Lang-Ho, took me one day to visit this privileged country, and while admiring the beauty of the landscape, I could not refrain from actions that showed clearly my surprise."

"In the gardens that surround the small houses, I see the blooming amaryllis opening its gorgeous chalices from which spring pollen-laden pistils, looking like a woman's long eyelashes that have been made heavy with paint; in the flowerbed bloom roses, delicate or pronounced indoors; while large convolvuli climb the roofs and fall in jagged clusters."

"The fields extend monotonously in the distance; strips of land were planted with solid banks of chrysanthemums, whose bitter odour we could plainly detect. But above all other odours arose the balsamic fragrance of the resinous trees, vivifying and persistent. Yet, although I looked around carefully, I could perceive no sign of those trees, whose odour filled our lungs."

"Then my master looked at me and smiled:'I thought that you would be surprised,' said he; 'that is the common experience of those that visit this country for the first time; but how few among them are wise enough to draw a lesson from what they observed.'"

"Pointing at a low hill, whose silvery verdure appeared to stand out like a luminous mass against a sky of tenderness blue, he continued: 'Look! Behind that light screen of bushes is a grove composed of resinous trees. We cannot see them, but their beneficent influence diffuses itself throughout the surrounding country. Do not neglect the lesson this teaches, my son! That little grove of regenerative power happily illustrates a man whose influence radiates upon and extends itself over those that approach him, in pouring out upon them the balm it distils.'"

"Just as the light and frivolous birches hide rough branches and roots whence proceed health and life, the art of influencing must learn how to surround itself with an aspect of amiability, and in order to reach men's souls, it must abandon the idea that it must be composed merely of the rougher and more rugged virtues, so much extolled by many philosophers."

"Influence must know how to enter the most thoughtless spirit, after the manner in which the balsamic odour penetrates these gewgaw little houses, with their gardens filled with useless flowers."

"Most invalids recoil at the mere notion of the boredom of living in the woods; but they come with pleasure to establish themselves among flowers, and yield unconsciously to the restoring influence that radiates around them in the vivifying balsamic atoms."

"With the coming winter they will depart. They will take

up their old way of life, detaching themselves completely from that which has given them a new birth, so to speak; but they will bear within themselves this principle of new life, which has implanted itself without their will, and which will by slow degrees develop itself in the form of a desire to return."

"Be not blind, my son, but receive seriously the lesson given to you by the immensity and simplicity of Nature. As she influences the body, know that she influences souls also; and your earthly sojourn should contribute to the instruction of a strong and supple race, whose power will assert itself throughout the centuries."

"That man never really dies who knows how to assume sufficient empire over others to be able to trace lasting marks of his energy and power over the minds of those who, under his influence, bend their steps toward the highest."

"While he discoursed," Yoritomo continued, "I glanced around mechanically and saw some of the inhabitants of these little pleasure houses. Some among them occupied themselves with light tasks of horticulture; others strolled about, chatting; the women, whom one could discern among the shadows of the terraces, were preparing tea with a cheerful rattle of cups; no one appeared to give a thought to the neighbouring grove, yet everyone felt its beneficent influence."

"An imperious and passionate desire arose within me to allow the expansion of the forces with energy, always working and always increasing, had put in my brain that their powerful rays might penetrate weak souls and temper them for the bitter struggle of existence by reawakening in them a resolution toward good and hatred of evil, simultaneously with the dauntless courage which is the keynote of all success based on noble ambitions."

A single word struck me in this last phrase of the Japanese

philosopher. He did not say "to create" but to "reawaken" in men's souls a resolution toward good and hatred of evil. It is only in the simplest romances and the most naïve plays that men are good or bad all in the same way, without any variation.

On the contrary, it is easy to show that each individual is a prey, at a given moment or in special circumstances, to contrary impulses that show in him the presence of a double sensibility.

We will not speak of inclinations that correct themselves or grow weaker after reflection; for example, the sudden and unlooked for prodigality of a miser who fancies he may gain something by a show of liberality; the voluntary self-indulgence of a man who knows how prejudicial to him may be an appearance of excessive strictness or severity; or the temporary abstemiousness of a gourmand who reserves his appetites for a feast.

Instinct more often takes the place of reason, in imposing on each person acts of contradictory sentiment, according to the time, the place, or circumstances.

Our mind is only too often the field of evolution wherein are elaborated resolutions that are not dictated by an attentive and conscientious will.

Our modern way of speech calls such persons impulsive; following the bend of the idea that haunts them, they may be heroic or cowardly, proud or servile, kind or cruel; it is often impossible for the observer, as well as for themselves, to determine the exact quality, whether good or bad, that plays the chief part in the character of the normal man.

"There are those," Yoritomo continues, "who, dazzled by the fantastic dreams of a theoretic existence, recoil before the effort necessary to reestablish themselves in actual life and in stripping the rags of illusion from their chimera."

"All those, again, whom inertia holds ensnared in their vices will feel their hearts moved by an emotion leading toward light and toward the practice of virtues, indispensable to him, who desires to face triumphantly the conflict of existence."

Note that the Shogun does not speak of "creating" the feeling that gives the impulse toward god; he wishes simply to awaken it, for he knows that it dwells within every heart. If it does not manifest itself, it is because the psychic qualities necessary to its production cannot create successfully the initial impulse, which fortified by the will and rendered more precise by concentration, will become efficacious in forming a habit.

But, in order to possess this gift in a way complete enough to exercise its beneficent influence over others, that it may be possible to suggest favourable thoughts and draw men back from the incline of baleful resolutions, it is indispensable that we should provide ourselves with that beneficent power which must radiate from ourselves as heat rises from a glowing hearth.

What must one do to gain this power? Listen again to the Shogun:

"We possess," said he, "innumerable forces that lie hidden within ourselves, though it would be easy to lead them, as the waters of a canal are conducted, to make them serve for the conquest of good, spiritual as well as corporeal."

"The existence of these forces cannot be doubted; they abide in a latent state in some persons and appear intermittently in others. It is the lack of domestication of these forces that causes the frequent and disconcerting plurality of the Ego."

"What can one think of a man who today commits a villainous crime and who tomorrow, in the same circumstances, will perform an act of devotion?"

"Thinkers have often deduced from this phenomenon the theory that in such a man slumbers different states of the soul, of which one under the influence of a momentary emotion, surges up to the exclusion of all others."

"These manifestations of the energies that are buried in the most profound depths of being are, unless they are concerned in our moral betterment, almost always regrettable because they are thoughtless, springing up incomplete and nearly always contrary to those designs which deliberate reason would help us to accomplish."

"It is wise to direct these efforts to a practical end, and not toward such realizations of which the accomplishment would give no virile satisfaction." Apropos of this, Yoritomo related the following little legend:

"Once upon a time lived a man who was in love with the queen of the clouds. His days were passed in contemplation of the skies; when the sun shone he was sad, but when clouds floated across the heavens like gray tatters he delighted himself with fancying that he could behold his chimera."

"She was very capricious, and rarely assumed the same aspect twice. But from time to time he recognized her in some flocculent mass, whereupon his heart would swell with joy."

"At last, he resolved to join her and in order to do so he fancied he must build a monumental stairway that would reach to the sky. So he set himself to work, interrupting himself only to lose himself in the contemplation of his ideal."

"Years passed; his hair grew gray, his hands and knees trembled, but, faithful at his task, he continued painfully to add one step to another."

"At last a day came when the tottering builder, struggling in anguish against approaching death attained his object; the stairway reached the clouds, from the midst of which his beloved leaned toward him."

"He climbed the last step and extended his lips to the

longed-for apparition. But he received only the kiss of the rain, which dropping slowly, bore with it the form on which he had doted so many years."

"Returning to earth, the man wept. He wept for his lost youth, the beautiful years that had gone, and above all for his strength wasted in sterile efforts, when he might have put it to magnificent use."

May not this little legend be the origin of the story from which our modern writers have drawn the figure of Pierrot enamoured of the moon. Are there not many persons who pass their lives in building by slow stages a stairway that leads nowhere, and who do not perceive the fact until the work is finished. The struggle for life becomes more and more arduous, and the power of our hidden faculties should expand in accordance with ever-growing necessities. It is time, then, to awaken the forces that lie dormant within us.

"But," someone may object at this appeal, "evil forces as well as good will be aroused, and the combat between them will be so much the stronger because we ourselves must direct it."

The old Japanese philosopher had foreseen this objection, and he said quietly:

"Why fear to reanimate all the possibilities that lie dormant in our natures?" "Is it not desirable to cultivate all plants indiscriminately?"

"There are those that are poisonous, true, yet even these are indispensable in the practice of medicine." "Large doses of certain drugs cause death; but, administered wisely with the hand of a skilful physician, they bring relief and very often a complete cure."

"The same may be said of many forces that are evil only because they are not disciplined."

"There is still a danger to avoid; that of failing to discern those who can make us mistake for virtues the evil qualities that are only deceptive copies of virtues."

"Just as certain poisonous vegetables resemble those that are edible and wholesome, just as certain flowers have the form and colour of those that are inoffensive, up to the point where only the initiated can detect the difference, there are failings, which, by their origin, resemble virtues of which they are really the direct opposite."

"But naturalists are not deceived; the poisonous plant is recognized by them in the midst of a hundred others, and if they gather it, it is only to extract its medicinal properties."

The philosopher, adept in researches touching suggestion, distinguishes still more rapidly the "enemy" forces that disguise themselves under an appearance of false virtue.

"He will separate pride form vanity, perseverance from obstinacy, gentleness from weakness; and, strong in this knowledge he will know how to gather and to infuse into weak souls the infinitesimal dose necessary to produce the auxiliaries to success."

I observed that this word "success" occurred frequently in the remarks of the Japanese philosopher. It was because it is the "Open Sesame" of the magic gates that lead to the domain so much desired.

Success! It is the fulfillment of one or of several desires, all-converging toward one end. It is the reason for living for those who wish to struggle for the conquest of Good—that Good which has a way of transforming itself and seems farther away as soon as one has grasped it.

For wise men know the inanity of the word "perfection"; perfection cannot exist, since it cannot be absolute and is always debatable, following the bent of differing tastes or the application of doctrines. Others, whose convictions modify the ideal, criticize a thing that seems to some persons the highest degree of Good will.

At this point Yoritomo, as he delighted to do, illustrated his words with a fable:

"A man once lived," said he, "who resolved to climb to the highest summit of a chain of mountains, so that no obstacle should hide from him the view of the universe.

"After countless fatigues, he climbed the peak which from below seemed to him higher than all the others; the ascent was rough, the road arduous and dangerous; but the man, possessed by his idea, felt neither the scorching sun which burned his face, nor the biting north wind on wintry nights."

"In order to avoid precipices and possible traps along the road, he walked with a bent head and did not raise it until the moment when his feet reached the lofty plateau, the object of his strenuous efforts."

"Alas! What disillusion was his! A granite wall, which clouds had heretofore hidden from his gaze on looking up from below, rose before him, straight, rigid, impracticable, as it seemed to him."

"Impracticable! Not entirely so, but perilous and above all mysterious, for the clouds that enveloped it hardly permitted him to discern the road that he must follow amid a thousand dangers."

"The man postponed the accomplishment of his desire. He descended into the valley again to wait for the dispersion of the clouds, so that he could choose his road by a clearer light."

"But that was not the real cause of his chagrin. The topmost peak was invisible from below, and he asked himself bitterly whether his great fatigue had not been caused by a mirage, after all."

"Should he begin another ascent? It was such hard work—it

was better to wait! Now that he knew from which side he should climb to reach the summit, there was no need to worry about it. Besides, did a summit really exist? And even if it did, might he not encounter, after a weary climb, still another eminence, which he had not yet been able to discern!"

"Days passed; the propitious moment did not present itself and at last the man died in the valley, having lived a life interwoven with regrets and aspirations the more cruel because he well knew that he had not the energy sufficient to satisfy them."

"This often happens to those that assign to themselves nothing short of perfection as the end of their efforts. As soon as they imagine they have attained it, they try sadly to ascertain whether there is not something more left to conquer."

"Those among them who have become wise compel themselves simply to attain the highest, and soon acquire a passionate enthusiasm for their task, for their aim is not circumscribed but grand and infinite."

"One should pity those who believe themselves to have 'arrived' quite as much as those who despair of arriving. The former, thinking they have nothing more to combat, soon come to believe that there is nothing more worth conquering."

"Combat increases our energies, and the desire to live become more determined when one fears that he must die before he has accomplished his task."

"But," asked someone, "when should one enjoy the benefits of his continued efforts?"

The answer was ready:

"From the perpetual pursuit of the highest springs a series of realizations, each of which gives us the joy and pride of conquest. Does a trader cease to do business because he has just made a good bargain? While he appreciates the advantages gained in the long-pursued transaction, he will enter upon another into which he will throw himself eagerly, and will even use the gains of the preceding bargain to make sure of negotiating the second."

"Thus we should use acquired forces, the advantages gained over ourselves in the realization of another ideal, which, once attained will allow us to pursue another of a form more nearly perfect."

"That man in whom moral strength grows and increases is very near decadence, and that means that he will enter on the road leading to shadows and death."

"Let us then turn resolutely toward the light; above all, let us increase our psychic forces, for they alone can give us that power that emanates from certain beings whose domination exercises itself beneficially over those that surround them."

"Just as when, in the heat of the sun, all grains and seeds sleeping in the earths bosom sprout and rise in the form of plants to play their part in the universal fete of Nature, so under the power of influence always augmented and disciplined by noble deeds the hearts of those near us will open to a desire for the best, conducive to the general aim of mankind—Happiness."

# 2

## BY PERSUASION

"Persuasion," Yoritomo taught us, "clothes itself in two very different forms; the one invades the soul like the invisible molecules of a soothing balm poured from a kindly hand and gently infiltrates itself throughout our systems, communicating to us its virtues. The other may be compared to the terrible wind of the African deserts."

"If, from the first hour one feels its burning touch, he has not known how to avoid it by shutting himself closely within his dwelling, every crevice and opening of which has been sealed, nothing can escape its attacks."

"The imperceptible sand drifts little by little into all corners of the house, and even reaches all parts of the human body."

"However well protected we may be, it even penetrates closed lips and eyes, and soon this almost invisible tinge seizes on every man and becomes his constant preoccupation. Evil persuasion is all the more dangerous because it knows how to clothe itself with the most attractive external attributes."

"That is what we meet in the guise of counsellors whose words are always tempting, since they adopt the false appearance of solicitude. With earnest words and sympathetic smiles, these persons who almost always have nothing to do in life, try to spoil the lives of others, without having a suspicion of their unconscious crime."

"Usually these are the kind of persons that talk in apparent good faith about the freedom to live one's own life. They are those who seek the agreeable sensation of the moment, without giving a thought to the possible bitterness of tomorrow."

"They have to learn harsh lessons, for all that; often they are compelled to suffer for days and weeks in order to pay for one day of careless pleasure; but these days are either soon forgotten or their lightness of character is such that they prefer to take the risk of drawing down on themselves serious troubles in the future than to make any effort in the present to avoid them."

Here Yoritomo, always ready with examples, related the following story:

"I once knew a young man, the son of one of my friends, who was afflicted with a certain lightness of judgement."

"He was not bad at heart, but his effeminacy and lack of strength of will made him an undesirable companion for such of his young friends whose souls were not sufficiently tempered by the practice of a continual appeal to dominating forces."

"One day he was calling on one of his friends whose father occupied an important place in the senate, and who sent his son to the house of one of his colleagues to learn the result of a discussion in which he had not been able to take part."

"Apropos of a very important question on which a favoured future or disgrace depended; he wished to know what a night session of the senate had determined."

"On the way, the son of the senator confided his apprehensions to his frivolous friend. To this young man these weighty matters seemed unimportant and childish, and he dwelt much on the bore it would be to allow this matter to spoil an evening in which both friends had promised themselves much pleasure."

"His reply filled the senator's son with consternation; the night session had taken place and the most important affairs had been discussed. His adversaries had attacked the absent senator with great bitterness."

"But the friend said, 'since the contretemps is sure to bring trouble and spoil the pleasure we were looking forward to, why risk this trouble. We can tell your father that the session did not take place, and that all is going well!'"

"The senator's son resisted; 'He would not dare lie to his father,' he said. But his friend became more insinuating: 'It would not be a serious lie, and besides, one would have time to say that some one had misunderstood—in fact, are we quite sure that there had not been some misunderstanding?'"

"In order to vanquish his friends last hesitations, the young gentleman pretended to recall the whole interview, analysing its details and inventing others. Meantime, he said they would say that several persons had stopped them and questioned them; was it not to one of these that they had replied?"

"He said so much in so persuasive a way that at last the senator's son deliberately told his father that the expected session had been postponed until the following day. Under the influence of this evil persuasion he felt not the slightest remorse in telling this falsehood, and passed a delightful evening."

"But alas! The next day must have been terrible. His father and his partisans could not be found at all in time to foil the scheme of his enemies; his disgrace was decided on, and the order to commit hara-kiri was sent to him."

"After he was dead, his effects were confiscated and his son dragged out the miserable existence of the poor being whom will and dignity do not console."

The old philosopher did not tell us whether the friend, the cause of all these disasters, sought to palliate them by coming to the aid of him whom he had ruined by his detestable counsel.

But it is probable that, feeling in this affair as those feel who are conscious of their contemptible conduct, he looked on indifferently at the misfortunes chargeable solely to his own lightness of character. It is, in fact, a common trait with those who are conscious of their own inability to make the least effort to experience a wicked sort of pleasure in observing the failure of others.

Another variety of the agents of bad persuasion is the persons we call pessimists, whom Yoritomo describes thus:

"One should flee those who are created with life which makes one think only of the stupor of death. Their souls are always in the state where one finds the body in the tomb; every effort seems useless to them, or rather, they prefer to make a show of that indifference which makes the gestures necessary to obtain the accomplishments they pretend to despise."

"Despise them indeed! Do they not feel rather a malicious joy in demoralizing others? They like to consider man as fundamentally bad, and to declare that the slumber of the dead is the superior of all other pleasures."

"That is true only regarding those who, as we have said, pass through life as if they were already dead. They would be right, perhaps, if one heard only through pleasures of the gross, earthly joys of existence."

"But, for those that know how to see, the joy of living is in all things, and we can taste it, even in the midst of the greatest afflictions."

"Can the grief of mourning, cruel though it may be, prevent us from admiring the sunshine at the moment when it hangs the purple of the sunset in the sky before it sinks to sleep behind the quivering birch trees!"

"Can any grief, whatever it may be, prevent us from feeling a delicate emotion on hearing the sweet, strong voice of a boatman, whose song is lost in the distance when his light craft disappears in the golden mist of the great lakes?"

"The joy of life throbs everywhere about us; it is in everything that surrounds us, and we should gather all our strength to cry out against those that preach pessimistic doctrine, for every life, sad thou it may be, is worth living."

Do we not hear those that talk about the scourge of our day, neurasthenia—which often is only one of the commonest forms of egoism for those that are attacked by it—refuse not only to believe in the beautiful and the good, but they devote the last sparks of their fast disappearing will to persuading others of the uselessness of everything?

Are they always sincere? Do they not do this in a sort of spite against those who are more expert in the art of living and who excite their envy by enjoying the blessings of life that their own moral weakness does not allow them to appreciate?

How much happier are those of who Yoritomo says:

"They accept joyfully the evil of living and show it in their fervent adoration of everything that is beautiful and good."

"These," he added, "are the true priests of favourable persuasion. They know by the authority of their own conviction, how to give courage again to the weak and faith to the incredulous."

"By the virtue of persuasion, they banish from the invalid the pains, which almost always hasten the apparition of imaginary sufferings. They know the right words to say to strengthen weak will and to give to those who suffer pain in reality the courage to support the ills which sympathy and solicitude made lighter. They are, in short, true healers."

"The persuasion toward health is the best of panaceas, for no one denies the influence of moral qualities on physical health. I once knew a man, who under the influence of one fixed idea, was about to die. He imagined that while drinking the water of a stagnant pool he had swallowed a serpent, minute at first, but which growing larger inside of his body caused internal ravages of which he felt himself likely soon to die."

"His friends had told me of his singular case, telling me how anxious they were at seeing this so-called invalid wasting away day by day. I was curious to visit him; I found a real invalid, looking very ill with features sunken and hardly able to drag himself about. Pressing his chest, he told us that the serpent was devouring him. His friends laughed at him and seemed to think that I would join them in their mirth, but I judged the moral evil too serious to try to soother him by trying to reason with him."

"Persuasion alone, based on a real or an imaginary proof, with the aid of suggestion could save the man. Instead of laughing with the others, I pretended to believe that he was really ill and asked him to tell me his story, to which I listened with the deepest attention. To his great astonishment, I sympathized with him in his trouble and spoke of one of my friends, a famous healer, who would be happy to interest himself in the invalid and to try to save him."

"Two days later I returned, actually bringing with me a physician whom I had told of this strange mania, and who had promised me his assistance. For it was indispensable to have near me someone who could speak authoritatively in order to impress the mind of the invalid. He examined the patient carefully, prescribed certain medicines, and withdrew without giving any words of positive hope."

"Then began my part, that of a psychologist. I pretended that I would tell him the absolute truth, however brutal it might seem. The doctor had discovered beyond all doubt the presence of the serpent; he had tried certain medication. Would it succeed? He dared not affirm it."

"Several days passed with alternating fear and hope, which

indications I noted carefully. Finally, one day the physician declared that he was about to make a decisive test of which he had great hope of a favourable result."

"I had known so well how to be persuasive and had understood so thoroughly how to surround the patient with the right occult influences that he no longer rejected the idea of a possible cure; and when, after taking certain medicines that induced him to vomit freely, we showed him the serpent which he believed he had thrown up, our invalid found himself suddenly cured."

"After this, if he happened to feel again pain or discomfort of any kind, he attributed it to the ravages caused by the serpent, and, as the cause existed no more the evil soon disappeared."

"This case shows that one of the conditions of succeeding in the art of persuading is not to batter rudely at convictions that one wishes to uproot. This hardly requires an explanation; in order to persuade some one it is necessary to merit his sympathy; now, one never gains the sympathy of those whose opinions he does not share."

"Hence, in order to persuade successfully, one must banish suspicion and know how to listen. One must not forget the profound egotism that characterizes all imaginary invalids; they are so full of themselves that their ills seem to them to acquire high importance."

"They cannot admit that the whole world is not interested in their aches and pains, and the importance they themselves attach to themselves is a subject of development for their malady. For it is incontestable that all moral emotion has an immediate repercussion on the physical state. To be able to persuade a patient that he is cured is, in most cases, to free him from his malady; it is always infinitely attenuated, since it is to spare him moral uneasiness, too fruitful mother of bodily ills."

But Yoritomo did not stop here with instructing us in the benefits of persuasion; he extended his remarks to the unfortunates who are assailed by the doubt even of happiness, and he encouraged them with this parable:

"A young lord was passing one day along the highroad when his palanquin struck so roughly that it was broken to pieces, he looked at the ruins a moment, then he ordered his bearers to go in search of a new one and sat down by the roadside to wait for them to bring it."

"A poor man passing by stopped and talked with him about the accident. 'And what shall you do with these pieces?' he inquired."

"'Why, nothing,' the rich man replied. 'I shall leave them where they are.'"

"'Then will you allow me to take them?'"

"'Yes, since I don't want them.'"

"The beggar then set himself to work; he readjusted the boards, washed the soiled spots on the hangings in the nearest brook, and did so much and so well that toward evening the palanquin, although a little deteriorated, it is true, was solid and fit to use again."

"Just then the bearers returned. They had not been able to find anything a palanquin so light and frail that, as soon as they tried it, they saw that it would not do."

"There the beggar intervened and offered 'his' palanquin. The young lord was glad to pay a large indemnity to have the use for several hours of a thing, which in reality belonged to him."

"And that," adds the old philosopher, "is the experience of many persons who will not understand that a destroyed happiness may prove a kind of blessing, if one knows how to gather up the pieces."

"Instead of grieving over them and abandoning them by

the wayside in order to wait for what may turn up, is it not better to do as the beggar did and to seek in the mishap a security which we should find it difficult to be sure of in the coordination of new events?"

"It is on such occasions as this that the power of influence comes into play. In order to persuade men that it is easier for them to work at the construction (or reconstruction) of the happiness that is near them, psychic power is more necessary than it is in drawing them into hypothetic adventures."

"Few men are not attracted by the magic of 'beginning over again,' and how many others count on luck, which they almost deify!"

"When can they convince themselves that, for those who know the power of influence, which develops a steady will and a strong thought, luck is born chiefly of circumstances created by ourselves? Almost always are the architects of our own fortunes; it is in working at them without respite that we may model them if not wholly according to our wish, at least in a way somewhat approaching it."

"It is by believing steadfastly that we shall attain the highest power, that we shall acquire the qualities that make a man almost more than man, since they allow him to govern and subdue those by whom he is surrounded."

Might we not say that here Yoritomo presented the "superman" of Nietzsche, and do we not find in all those theories a commentary on the modern phrase of power of mind over matter?

In what manner does this evolution produce itself and above all by what means can one obtain these quasi-miracles? How does one make this effort to attain the desired end, and what qualities, occult or material are necessary to develop to attain this magnificent ambition to conquer the minds of men? Listen to what the Shogun tells us in the following chapters.

# 3

## THE INFLUENCE OF THE EYES

Few people escape the influence of the human eye. If its look is imperious, it subjugates; if it is tender, it moves; if it is sad it penetrates the heart with melancholy.

But this influence cannot be real and strong unless it is incited by the thought behind it, which maintains and fixes that look, in communicating to it the expression, terrible or favourable, persuasive or defiant, which alone can maintain the firmness and the perseverance of the active forces of our brain.

"Some persons," said Yoritomo, "possess naturally a fascinating eye; usually they are those who can maintain a steady gaze for a long time without blinking."

"But it is not sufficient to be able to throw a glance the persistence of which sometimes causes a passing discomfort, which almost always tends toward the subjection of spirits of the weaker sort."

"This look should be the projection of a thought in which the fixed form is definite enough so that its penetrative influence shall become efficacious."

"But," someone will say, "it is not always necessary to think, since several animals possess this power of fascination, like the snake, which holds a bird motionless under the power of its gaze, so that it never dreams of trying to use its wings to escape from its enemy."

"But if conscientious thought does not exist in the animal, it is nevertheless active in responding to instinct."

"There is a blind force in the brain of the serpent, and which turns it from taking possession of its prey, and this force, mastered by a powerful instinct determines a compulsion, which in the weaker creature is sufficient to paralyse all inclination to resist."

But the serpent does not monopolize this privilege of fascination, if one may believe certain old French chronicles.

In the old book published by Rousseau in the seventeenth century, it is related that a toad, shut up in a vase, could not get out and found it difficult to endure the fascination of the human eye; at first, in evident uneasiness, it tried to escape; then, when convinced that that was impossible, it would return to its former position and stare at the person in its turn, and ended by dying of the effect of this peculiar force. Is it necessary to lend strength to this story by adding that one day a toad, stronger or more irritable than the others, riveted its eyes so long upon a mans eyes that he actually felt the influence of the creature and swooned under the implacable fixity of its gaze?

I do not believe that such experiences have been officially established, but it is nonetheless interesting to conclude that if under the sway of an instinctive thought, the eye of an animal can acquire a rare power. The eye of man, when he is animated by an active reasonable thought, may be an important agent of influence of suggestion.

"In order to convince an adversary," said the Japanese philosopher, "one must look him straight in the eyes. But it would be very stupid and unskillful to employ this method without discretion."

Some would see in it only insolence, and their irritation would prevent them from feeling the full influence of the gaze; others would feel a certain uneasiness which would cause them to turn the eyes away before having submitted entirely to the gazer's influence, and might prevent them from renewing an interview with a person that had impressed them so unpleasantly.

The best way to begin the use of the eye in influencing is to talk of subjects that will not arouse suspicion in the interlocutor.

One should present himself in an easy and quiet manner listen without showing any signs of impatience of whatever objections the person may make; some of these may not be lacking in accuracy, and it would be unwise to combat them.

It is unnecessary to add that the least hastiness, which would displace the point of concentration of the thought, would be injurious and might work serious harm to the success that we seek.

Too great excess of modesty should be avoided, for the transmission of thought—and consequently of influence—is worked at our cost.

Timidity is always an obstacle to the influence of the eye, which should, at the very first interchange of glances look straight and frankly into the eyes of the interlocutor, at the top of the bridge of the nose. The first conflict once over, one should turn away his eyes carelessly; especially he should avoid the eyes of his opponent (as we will call him) in the first minutes of conversation, before your own have gained any hold on him; one should in some way fix his gaze without allowing his eyes to gain a hold over your own.

In short, he who wishes to influence another by his look, must take the greatest care not to let him suspect his design, which would immediately put him on the defensive and render all your efforts vain.

"I once knew a young man named Yon-Li," added Yoritomo, "who went to call on a Daimio to conclude a transaction that was injurious to his own interests."

Besides, the friend had promised a round sum to Yon-Li if he should succeed in influencing this important person to the point of accepting this solution.

For a long time the young man had practised exercises in the development of psychic influence and believed that he had arrived at the point when one is sure of himself.

He entered and immediately threw on the Daimio a glance, which the other thought rather singular; he tried to surmise the cause of a look, which became almost aggressive in its expression of determination to dominate him.

He was a man of strong will, who had for a long time exercised his powers of penetration.

He had no great difficulty in discovering the motive that actuated the young Yon-Li, and he conceived the idea of fighting him with his own weapons.

Taking care to avoid looking into the pupils of his visitor's eyes, he fixed him in the way which we have described, concentrating his gaze at the top of the bridge of the nose and strongly centring his thought on the idea of domination.

The young amateur was not prepared to meet an attack more powerful than his own; his bold assurance faltered a little; under the influence of that penetrating look he blinked, lowered his eyelids, and gently turned away.

He was vanquished and it was with hesitation that he made his request. It was not entertained or even listened to, and he had besides the embarrassment of confessing, despite himself, the indelicate step which he had been ready to undertake.

Yoritomo added:

"The influence of the eye is undeniable; it is occult power set in vibration by the force of the thought; it is the result of the action of the forces that surround us, combined with our own vital force."

"One should not use these forces by chance. It is well to use them, especially, as arms, offensive or defensive, in the great battle won by wisdom and knowledge of human nature."

But just as when he instructed us in the acquiring of energy, as well as when he taught us how to overcome timidity, Yoritomo did not content himself with uttering precepts; he told us the methods whereby we might acquire the precious gifts that he extolled.

"In order to attain that authority of the eye which is one of the first conditions in the study of acquiring mental dominance," said Yoritomo, "certain exercises are necessary":

"For example, it is well to lay a stick of bamboo across a sheet of vellum, and then sear oneself at a few steps' distance and stare fixedly at the bamboo without allowing the eye to wander to the sheet of vellum. One must use all his strength of will to avoid blinking."

"This exercise should begin with counting up to twenty, then to thirty, increasing the enumeration up to two hundred, which is enough. When one can perform this first exercise easily, it will be time to pass to another, a little more complicated."

"Having made a hole in the sheet of vellum—taking great care to pierce it in such a way as to have the edges of the opening neat and clean-cut, experimenter now rivets his fixed gaze on this aperture one, two, three minutes, longer if possible."

"It is well also to place oneself in front of a bright, smooth surface, preferably polished tin—lacking one silver or gold—and to seek in it the reflection of his own eyes."

"Plunge your gaze into the inmost depths of your eyes; from the beginning this will be a good exercise in compelling the gaze of others the yield to your own."

"In this situation, turn the head from the right to left, then from left to right, without losing sight one's glance firmness and the desired power. One should avoid winking the eyes and lowering the eyelids, and should practice meeting firmly the gaze of others."

But all these exercises would be in vain, if during the time of this contemplation, you do not know how to concentrate your mind on a single subject. How much influence could you exercise over others if you do not know first how to master yourself?

Singleness of thought is indispensable during the development of the use of the eye; if it seems too difficult to keep it fixed on a single point, it would be well to avail oneself of certain means of suggestion, like the following:

"First, count up to ten with the simple idea of doing it slowly, and to allow the same space of time to elapse between the uttering of each number."

"Secondly, run through the fingers a chaplet of about sixty beads, counting them in a low tone of voice, without losing sight of the point one has fixed on."

"One may count at first up to five or ten; then increase the count, taking care to begin all over again if one finds one's attention has wandered or that while pronouncing the numbers it has been diverted, of only for an instant, from the single thought that is the object of his purpose."

But this is not all; as soon as one has acquired the desired qualities in the cultivation of the power of the eye, he should begin to experiment with them, and regarding this here is what our philosopher counsels us:

"When you have mastered the use of the eye, and have learned how to concentrate the mind, try the ascendancy of your visual power on some person in the midst of a crowd."

"First, choose some one whose face indicates a character weaker than your own, and fix your gaze in the back of his neck, with a single thought, which shall invade his mind, haunting him with a desire to turn around."

"If your influence is already sufficiently formed, at the end of a certain time you will see him begin to fidget, then to move his head slightly, as if to shake off an importunate thought; finally, he will move his hand to the spot on which your gaze has been fixed, then, in spite of himself he will turn around."

"This experiment may be made on all sorts of subjects, and it will always succeed on condition that you know how to envelope your subject in and intense mental current the action of which will combine itself with the power of your gaze."

"You can imagine, then, to what extent this faculty may be useful in the ordinary circumstances of life; it is the secret of those we call fascinating persons, whom no one can resist and who know how to obtain anything they desire by merely saying what pleasure it would give them to possess the desired object; for they know well that in concentrating that mind strongly on that for which they ask, the mind of their interlocutor, yielding to mental sway, abandons itself easily, especially if the domination of the eye increases this conviction by creating in him a psychic state which compels him to submit to its power." These precepts were those of that other tamer of spirits, Mahomet, who said:

"The effect of the human eye is indubitable. If there is anything in the world that can move more rapidly than fate, it is the glance of the eyes."

From this saying strong superstitions have arisen, against which the Shogun puts on our guard:

"One of the reasons," says he, "that militate in favour of the cultivation of the influential use of the eye is the necessity of getting the better of a certain kind of persons who pretend to have inherited occult power from magicians."

"A man gifted with a strong will has nothing to fear from

these shameless liars; but a sensitive and impulsive person, who does not know how to assert himself and dominate others, becomes an easy prey, and the suggestions of these wretches will soon lead him to dissipate his fortune in answering their stupid requests."

"Besides," Yoritomo added, "those that would wish to use their occult influence to compel others to commit a wrong action would be soon punished by the loss of this influence, which develops itself gently only when actuated by beneficent thought; while they retract and end by becoming annihilated when the uppermost thought is of the kind of which may be said:

"'Evil thoughts about others are rods with which we ourselves shall one day be beaten.'"

# 4

## THROUGH CLEARNESS OF SPEECH

The word is the most direct manifestation of the thought; hence it is one of the most important agents of influence when it clothes itself with precision and clearness, indispensable in cooperating in creating conviction in the minds of one's hearers.

Were not the burning words of Peter the Hermit the sole cause of the rising of arms for the conquest of the tomb of Jesus? And was it not especially because that monk believed himself firmly to be moved by a divine will that he knew how to make his belief shared by thousands of men of all classes, poor or rich, who under the influence of his words all possessed only a single soul, impregnated with sentiments of heroic piety which urged them to dye the sands of Palestine with their blood?

What arguments had this monk found? Only three words, but powerful words, when one considers the mentality and the peculiar religiosity of that epoch: "God wishes it!"

"God wish it!" These words were the first to declare to the ignorant masses Peter's all-powerful influence. In the eyes of the vulgar, this man who transmitted to them thus the will of the Most High assumed in their eyes the proportions of a divine messenger, a sort of prophet in communication with the Master of Masters, who designed to dictate to him His orders.

For others, it was to resume debates by an argument without reply; it was to excuse fatigues and privations and an unknown death under a foreign sky. God wished it! How vain were all other speeches after these three words, which bowed all heads under the powerful breath of divine domination, as wheat bends under the tempestuous winds!

Yoritomo speaks as a true sage, then, when he says:

"Leaders of souls should not forget this one thing: Too great wealth of words is hostile to conviction." And, alluding to a Japanese proverb, which is very similar to one of our own well-known proverbs, he added:

"If speech is like jade, silence is like a diamond."

"Speech is like a diamond when it is the vibrating form of the concrete thought and when it presents itself in a quiet way, rendering its suggestions familiar and clear by the way in which the orator knows how to present them."

"Prolific speech is the medium of powerful thought—of that thought of which we should be master and not slaves."

"Speech is the seed, good or ill-omened, which, sown in irresolute natures, may produce either nettles or wheat."

This may be also the "fixed idea" that is supposed to be implanted in every weak brain. Suppose someone should chance to being endowed with the power of initiative, but with a wavering will:

"You will be good, because goodness is the supreme end of life. If the order is accompanied by the dominating look of which we have spoken and pronounced in a tone that will impress, there is no doubt that these influences will produce such a radiation as, in spite of himself, would make him feel himself under the influence of good emanating from himself to converge toward his fellows."

"This may seem very obscure at first, but the brevity and precision of order will implant themselves little by little in his brain, of which the passive forces, always submissive to confused influence, will at a certain moment determine the active forces to emerge from the background where up to then they had lain hidden."

"But if one expresses this prophecy some day before being afflicted with moral weakness: 'You will be a criminal,' the idea, originally repelled with horror, ends by sowing in his brain an idea first of the impossibility of the suggestion, then, more frequently evoked it become less monstrous and he finishes with a smile of doubt at the beginning, then with fear, by facing the eventuality of this prophesied crime, the specter of which had pursued him so persistently, that one day, when carried away by anger or violent passion, he accomplished this criminal act against the temptation of which he would certainly have reacted, had he not been possessed with the fixed idea which designed him before his own eyes as the instrument predestined by Fate."

"That is the reason why," added the Shogun, with infinite wisdom, "one cannot blame too much such parents as the prophesy for their children terrible punishments for reprehensible acts which they can hardly help committing."

And he added:

"Those who, thinking to cure their children of faults more or less characteristic, repeat to them: 'You will die under the executioner's whip,' are sometimes the involuntary cause of this execution."

"To strengthen this idea of so lugubrious a fate for the little ones, they familiarize them with it, and dwell on its horrors."

"Then they compromise constantly their authority before their children, for they, seeing them the next day filled with kind feelings and expressing tenderness toward them, will not fail to regard lightly the terrible menace with which they were threatened."

"It might happen that they were struck by it, and that would be likely to be unlucky for their future, for, once implanting this idea in their brains, they will not fail to wonder at the serenity of their parents, who can admit the possibility of so terrible a fate and yet go on living peacefully with the menace of such a future for their child."

"In every way, the authority of the heads of the family will find itself lessened, and the seed sown in the heart of the child by the imprudent prophecy cannot fail to produce bad fruit."

"It will be so much the more dangerous if it should be resumed in a few words, those incisive words that draw mental pictures, which take root in the brain."

"Long lectures have only a repressing effect on the spirit."

"One's listeners, endowed with will and discernment, very soon give up trying under the avalanche of words that fall on their ears with the monotony of flakes of snow, to distinguish truths that are uttered in the confused mass of verbiage."

"On the contrary, they force themselves to turn these thoughts from this wordy chaos, in which the confusion equals the monotony."

"As for others, the laxity of their attention does not permit them to follow the same idea very long, and, all effort being painful to them, they will not long follow the orator in the mazes of thought through which he would conduct them."

"But those that know how to present their thoughts in a few phrases, in a way that impresses itself on their listeners, may easily become leaders of the masses."

"The first quality of the speaker who would be convincing should be to think deeply of what he wishes to say."

"As soon as he knows how to transform his thoughts into clear-cut images, the contours of which will not admit of any ones divining one line to be different from the line intended, he will be careful to project them into the minds of others under the form of lights and shades."

"We have already seen how the power of thought has the gift of influencing others, particularly when this force is aided by the power of the eye; when these two ruling faculties are augmented by the power of spoken discourse, the listeners are conquered by the ideas that are presented to them."

"Those who will acquire these gifts will find that he can interest men and attach them to himself; in a word, can lead them by the means of the influence that will assure him of mental empire over most of his contemporaries."

"It is necessary, also," the Shogun continued, "to base oneself on the theory of like attracts like, in the expansion of the sympathetic radiation which must converge toward great numbers to illumine men's souls."

"It has been remarked with what facility people follow noble impulses, heroic appeals, and generous outbursts."

"A speaker would be culpable, then, should he count on the inferior mental quality of his auditors in order to descend to their level."

"This is the fault of too many speakers who like to court less noble sides of the popular spirit."

"They give as a reason—I would almost say an excuse—that to address them in this way one is better listened to and more readily understood."

"This is a gross error. How many times have I uttered a noble thought in the midst of an assemblage of persons of mental mediocrity!"

"As this thought was always expressed in language clear and exact, formed of words that all could comprehend, every time I have had the pleasure of seeing the multitude vibrate like a harp struck by an expert hand, and to feel for a moment that the souls of the roughest of palanquin-bearers were elevated under the influence of my words which were adapted to the purest ideal."

"Is not this a kind of conquest for which those have devoted themselves to the art of influencing should strive?"

"It is by speech that one develops emotion, generator of noble gestures and of generous realization."

"Speech is the distributor of the thoughts that surround us, of which the reiterated suggestions, after impregnating certain groups of cells in our brain, travel, by affinity, to haunt the same group of brain-cells in other auditors."

"This is one reason why it is not well to dwell too long on the same subject, so that one can allow some rest to the weaker brains in an audience."

"Still, it is an undoubted fact that to jump from one subject to another, and to leave them only to attack them again, as is the custom of some speakers, is more fatiguing and less satisfactory, for minds wearied by this continual exercise end by ceasing to follow the flight of these fugitive thoughts; and, after waiting in vain for some repose in a discourse, they give up trying to follow the constant flight of too soaring imagination."

"Another type to be dreaded, are those devoted to idle chatter and gossip."

"One might, if he were greatly in earnest, correct them in this way: listen to their conversation, summarize it, and in ten minutes repeat to them all that had taken them an hour to say; by 'all' one must understand merely the ideas and not the repetitions."

"But will they stand correct? Will they not do as did a certain lord who, having seen his neighbour very ill, and having talked incessantly while visiting him without letting the sick man get a word in edgewise, said, when leaving him."

"I will return tomorrow to learn how you are, for I fear I have tired you very much because I have done so much talking today."

"Conciseness and clearness in speaking is thus a great force in the work of influencing, which is a noble task for one who undertakes it seriously."

"Moderation must be among the qualities whose aim is to action by the word in order to direct the focus of attention toward the principal thought which, excluding all accessory thoughts, should be imposed on the minds of his auditors by the speaker that wishes to extend his influence over them."

"Discretion is equally indispensable in forming influence by speech."

"From indiscretion to lying the step is short, and one should not forget this axiom that might be written in characters of jade on leaves of purest gold."

"Lying is a homage which inferiority renders unconsciously to merit."

"Bands of precious metals should be hung on the walls of salons, replacing, in a way more comprehensible to all minds, the covered rose-filled vases that ornament festal tables."

And Yoritomo reminded us of that ancient custom, which we believed peculiar to the Grecian sages, and which, it appears, was begun centuries ago among the philosophers of the Far East:

"Harpocrates, the god whom the ancient Greeks worshiped under the image of silence, had presented to the God of Love a flower which, coming from his hands, represented the virtue which he was supposed to symbolize."

"This gift was made in order to encourage the wanton boy to guard the secrets of his mother, Venus, for we know that Love was always ready to reveal the secrets of those that were attacked by his flames."

"This act of the god was imitated first by the Grecian sages, then by the Japanese philosophers; and at all banquets appears a closed vase, the cover of which must not be lifted."

"This vase encloses the roses, whose perfume filters through the interstices of the vessel, letting one guess what flowers are within."

"It was a custom to ask the guests to let nothing transpire regarding the discussions that took place in these gatherings."

"Later the custom became general and was followed among ordinary people, and then followed among ordinary people, when the closed and flower-filled vase was a constant warning to the guests to use discretion, and not to allow escaping outside anything that might have been said under the influence of wine."

"Our modern humour has immortalized this custom in the form of a figure of speech that is on everybody's tongue, but of which few persons know the origin, people often say of one who tells secrets: 'He has uncovered the rose jar!'"

The etymology of this figure is known to few, but however that may be, we are grateful to Yoritomo for recalling it to us by connecting it with one of the lessons he has taught us, which, disguised in the form of a parable, fix them in our minds in so attractive a fashion that we do not forget them as soon as we have heard them.

# 5

## BY SETTING GOOD EXAMPLE

"We read in a Japanese story that once a man set out in pursuit of a rose, he sought it a long time, but nothing seemed to him to be that flower, which he knew only by hearsay, that praised its incomparable perfume and the beauty of its multiplex corolla."

"He saw the admirable amaryllis, balancing on flexible stems their odoriferous chalices, whose tender tints were touched with brown spots, that seemed like the tears of night."

"He had inhaled—quite surprised to find them without perfume—the breath of the proud peonies, which bloomed near by, looking like a sort of burning bush."

"The fragrant stalactites of the acacias had breathed upon him their balmy odour."

"He had paused before carnations, which, crimson in their green chalices, looked like the throats of warriors, bursting out of their armour."

"The sumptuous mourning of the black lily also had attracted him; but none of these flowers were, nor could be, the rose, and he was almost in despair when he saw, quite near him, alight on a bush a butterfly of the dazzling colours, and a delightful aroma seemed to be diffused from it, while its wings quivered like the petals of a flower shaken in the wind."

"Greatly moved," the man approached it, saying: 'No,' said the butterfly, "I am not the rose, but I live near the rose; I love the refuge of her flowery arches and branches. I come to sleep in the hollows of her corollas, and sip the sweet perfume of her flowers."

"That is the reason why I have become so thoroughly impregnated with her odour as to deceive you."

This little fable may serve as a preface to anything one might say or write on the force of example. Our most frequent associations are never indifferent to our mentality, and we always submit, voluntarily or unconsciously, to the ascendancy of those that surround us, unless we have sufficient influence over their minds to compel them to submit themselves to us.

Then the thought, projected into an enveloping centre by a superior influence, is received by brains of weaker caliber, which register it mechanically in order to reproduce it on similar occasions.

Our popular modern philosophy has put this maxim into a proverb: "Tell me who are your associates and I will tell you what your are."

It is explained also by Du Potet in his "Magnetic Therapeutics..."

"There are certain persons," says he, "who when near you, seem to draw something from you, to pump you, to absorb your force and your life; an species of vampire, without knowing it, they live at your expense."

"When near them, in the sphere of their activity, one feels an uneasiness, a constraint which is caused by their pernicious actions and determines in us an indefinable feeling."

"You are moved by a desire to escape and to go far away from them; but these people have quite the opposite tendency; they come nearer and nearer to you, press close to you, seem fairly to wish to join themselves to you, to draw from you that which is necessary to their lives."

"Other persons, on the contrary, bear with them life and health."

"Wherever they go, they seem to radiate joy and sunshine."

"You observe that their conversation pleases and that people seek them out. One likes to touch their hands, to lean on their arm; something soothing which charms and magnetizes you, quite unconsciously, seems to emanate from them."

"One easily adopts their point of view on things in general, and their opinions, without knowing why; and one sees them go away with sincere regret."

In short, above all things regarding psychic influence, we must not forget that "the strongest reason is always the best."

Unfortunately, the strongest is not always that which is worth the most; a regrettable contagion follows from the person who suffers the ascendancy of the other.

"Or again," the old Shogun explained, "the reciprocal influence which individuals exercise on one another is the cause of many evils difficult to conjure."

"That, if we may believe tradition, is the reason why the sages of old created so-called mutual admiration societies, to which only those of undisputed merit were admitted."

"In the numerous reunions, whatever might be the apparent reason for them, a low mentality evinced itself, and the general quality of thought became inferior, to such a degree that the most elevated mind felt the difficulty of escaping the contagion of the surrounding mediocrity."

"The only influence of an orator might be to transmute souls momentarily by substituting for mean and niggardly thoughts a current of broad, generous ideas, from which would spring an enthusiasm real but almost always ephemeral, for at the moment of realization particular interests, narrow views, and the fear of responsibility will give back to each one of his auditors the mind that belongs to him, which a profound study of the attainment of the highest and best alone could transform slowly and definitely."

"However, certain such circles do exist which are composed of persons of absolutely pure aspirations, all communicant toward a noble end, in a collective thought, the waves of which are voluntarily directed toward a single accomplishment."

From these reunions of the best minds emanates a current of influence the value of which is considerable, since emulation, the offspring of example, is found in these circles where, each one developing, in a sense, from the same principle, concentrates his faculties on the search for the best in all that is good.

"But it is very difficult to maintain these gatherings under the unique direction of the original generous spirit. To find men that will ignore questions of temporary supremacy and of particular interests, and that know how to repress petty antipathies and hatreds, possibly more or less justifiable, in order to open the heart to the creation of an ideal—this is almost to expect the impossible."

"Is it, indeed, necessary to ask it? Is it well to suppress ambition in men's hearts? Does not such a leveling tend to destroy the seed of individual responsibility, a cognizance of which leads to the most noble conquests?"

While admiring the scruples of the Shogun, we could only regret that happy time when the ancient sages gathered with no other object than to talk of beauty in the heart of nature, in wonderful gardens in the midst of vegetation luxuriant and restful, with the blue heavens as their sole canopy.

But our modern civilization has other necessities, which find expression in a care, sometimes exaggerated, regarding subjection to the order of the hour: "Time is money"; it is necessary, then, that the time of the reunions should be limited, and that the place be carefully chosen, large enough to contain the public, which rarely would wish to assemble out of doors, lest the fine weather might change into a driving rainstorm.

The terrible question of money almost always comes up; and since persons of lofty minds, protagonists of generous ideas, rarely devote themselves to the accumulation of gold, it is necessary to introduce into these reunions a sort of Mecaenas who, under the guise of one or of several capitalists, whose ideas and sentiments may be said to border on the commonplace, comes among a group composed of the purest elements to play the part of fruit of doubtful quality in a basket of sound fruit.

But it is of no use regretting things that cannot be changed; and it is wiser to listen to Yoritomo: "I once knew a man who spent large sums in entertaining several Buddhist priests, who celebrated the cult by lighting an enormous quantity of lanterns, and by giving themselves up to various ruinous practises."

"I said to this man: 'It would be better to burn a single lamp before the statue of Buddha at his own home, and to invite all the priests who lead a useless existence in the temple to bear the people the good word and to set them a good example.'"

"Put together all the money which every year you would give to this sterile cult of Buddhism, divide it into as many sums as you would distribute to each of your priests in ordering them to distribute among the poor in teaching them the blessing of the name of Buddha."

"Thus, glorified by example, the cult that you desire to honour would spread itself the more, since kind and charitable words would inevitably be connected with it in the minds of the unfortunates whom it had helped."

We may, even now, take account of the strength of Yoritomo's principles in the observation that they are given as an example by another Japanese philosopher, Kabira Ekken, who lived in the seventeenth century, and of whom Kirschbach tells us in a study that is much quoted:

"The ability of certain actors," Yoritomo continued, "may be an influence, excellent or detestable, following the quality of the examples which they offer to the people."

"On the stage, an actor who has the gift of filling his very soul with the personage he represents can, at his will, sow the seeds of joy or terror, of admiration or desire for the beautiful in the minds of the spectators."

"That is the reason why we cannot too strongly reprehend such plays as show a narrow or vulgar mentality behind them."

"It is very wrong to impress the multitude with reproductions of criminal or reprehensible actions."

"While it is true that there are certain lower functions of our human nature that are common to every one, but which we mutually conceal, both from sight and by name, there are certain moral defects, certain ugly actions, a manifestation of which it would be very wrong to present to the eyes of the public."

"The acts of generosity, of magnanimous impulses, and of heroic sacrifices—do not these offer a field wide enough so that it is not necessary to reproduce plays of sentiments and actions that are likely to be harmful?"

"The influence of example is considerable, and it is a culpable thing not to circumscribe it to the representation of noble actins worthy of being imitated."

"It may be objected that in all plays in which a criminal is represented, the malefactor is always punished for his misdeeds, sometimes in a way so terrible that the example cannot fail to be of benefit as a warning to those that might be tempted to imitate him."

"Among an audience capable of being influenced by these

detestable examples, there are sure to be a few who will fancy themselves much cleverer than the criminal whose story is being acted before them, and these will say to themselves: 'This crime was well-planned; and, if he was taken, it is because he was clumsy.'"

"For many, these reflections are theoretical, and they have no desire to imitate him. But what matters then? The evil seed has been sown in them and, under the influence of an unworthy sentiment, hatred, calculation, or cupidity, it may develop into a fixed desire for dishonest conquest, of which the pictured crime was the origin."

"For those who are already tainted, the influence of such representations as we are considering would be even more vicious; for them the stage would be a practical school of vice, combined with astuteness and safeguarded from punishment by a thousand means which the actions of the players may suggest."

"One may say the same thing of books, though they are more dangerous for the erudite than for persons whose knowledge is more limited."

Alas! The Shogun knew nothing about compulsory education, for of the thousands of cheap books, which propagate the taste for trying one's luck in the convincing tone of showing one how to make a fortune. But it would be wrong to include the spirit of a book, which deplores all progress, which we praise highly. We should, however, emphasize very clearly the fact that too wide an education is often a two-edged weapon.

The best way to utilize one's education is to read attentively, "The Influence of Example."

Readings made in common should be on a subject at once lofty and interesting; but the result on the auditors when they are alone may be indifferent or beneficial, according to the mental qualities of the reader.

He should, above all things, be inspired with the principal contents of the preceding chapters, particularly those on the influence of the eye and thought-transference.

If the play of glances is necessarily limited to the reader, who is compelled to lower his eyes upon his book, he must not forget, in moments when he may be relaxing his gaze from the page, still to dominate his audience with his regard.

At the same time, the ideas he expresses should be backed by so powerful a thought from him that the "thought-waves" shall determine the mental current, which says Turnbull, "act with the force of a loadstone and of electricity."

Let us not forget also that personal influence radiates more certainly when it manifests itself under the form of altruism, charity, and kindness.

"Is it not a frequent thing," said the old Japanese, "to see a crowd hesitate, divided between a feeling of recrimination and one of approbation, and then suddenly turn toward conciliation, because one among them, on whom the situation and the influence of others had its effect, has openly declared himself on that side?"

"One of the greatest obstacles to the doing of good actions," he added, "is the timidity based on the fear of responsibility, which haunts mediocre minds."

"It is toward these that he who would wield the power of domination should turn his attention. It is sufficient to impose on these timorous souls the resolution to perform the task that they themselves desire to see accomplished, and to set them the example of his achievement."

"Their vacillating will strengthen itself by the moral support which they will be certain to feel, and their anxiety about the opinion of others will be soothed by the example of those whom they recognize as their superiors, and whose superiority they are glad to acknowledge."

"Example is the excuse behind which hasten to hide those whose ill—regulated thoughts can cooperate in defensive discernment."

"It is these, then, whose minds are strengthened by renewed practises of wise reflection, used in the service of psychic qualities, creators of domination, who should watch carefully over their own acts, so that their example may be, for the persons over whom they have an influence, a source of improvement and constant elevation."

# 6

## BY PSYCHIC INFLUENCE

Psychic influence consists in awakening the forces, too often wasted by a habitual state of moral weakness, or perhaps lessened from a physiological cause. It is the power that determines the processes, which we wish to produce in other minds.

It is the art of substituting for the want of resolution in others our own will, which they obey blindly, sometimes unconsciously, ever glad to feel themselves guided and directed by a moral power which they cannot elicit in themselves.

"It is not necessary," says Yoritomo, "to have as many pretend, recourse to magic, in order to become past masters in the art of influencing our fellows; what is needed above all is to keep ourselves constantly in a condition of willpower sufficient to impose our commands on minds capable only of obedience."

"Intensity of determination, when it reaches a certain point, possesses a dazzling influence which few ordinary mortals can resist, for it envelops them before they are aware of it and thus before they have dreamt of endeavoring to withdraw themselves from it."

"Moreover, the man who retains the power of influencing rarely needs to exert himself, in order to exercise it effectually, for the need of protection from it is non-existent in most persons."

"They are rare who are morally sufficient for themselves and who pass through life without feeling the need of resting their weakness on a supporting and directing force."

"Still less numerous are those who accept with courage the consequences of their acts and do not seek to place the responsibility for these acts on an outside influence, which, however, they are ready to repudiate if they're successful."

"But, should failure come, they will hasten to ascribe the causes to their advisers, proclaiming loudly that, if they had not been impelled to give ear to them, the disaster would not have come about."

"Timidity, while not influenced by the same motives, often leads those who suffer from it to such a dread of responsibilities that they arrive at the point of being unable to at, except under the shelter of an impelling power, the manifestation of which seems to them indispensable for excusing their activities."

"We might well pass over in silence persons of had faith, although they constitute an important group among those who seek the cooperation of others."

"But this sickly dependence on others is with them only adopted by design."

"Feeling themselves incapable of achieving anything by their own efforts."

"They're content to enjoy the fruit of the exertions of others, for they can always take credit to themselves for the best part, by throwing into the shade those who have a far better right to commendation than themselves."

"I once knew two brothers who were devoted to the study and explanation of the ancient inscriptions graven in temples by the hand of primitive faith."

"The younger of these brothers was verbose, very superficial, but a very brilliant and learned talker."

"The other, continually engrossed, kept himself almost

entirely out of sight, uttered only words absolutely necessary, and, when questioned on his science, replied so simply that people pitied his brother for being burdened with such an obvious nonentity."

"The latter, however, won the good graces of every one by never speaking of his elder brother except with respect and by displaying certain uneasiness when his learning was discussed."

"In spite of everything, he was obliged to admit he alone was learned, and his brother too shallow to take any other role that that of copyist; but it was perceived that this declaration hurt his brotherly feelings, and the esteem conceived for him increased the more."

"Now the day came when the elder brother vanished into the spirit world, his death passed almost as unnoticed as his life, and no one dreamt of regretting him, when a serious mistake was discovered in a much disputed text. Of course, the error fell on the memory of the copyist, that useless person whom the kindness of his brother had wished to class among the learned."

"The survivor appeared so affected by this that he gave up his work for some time, and his utterances grew dull and commonplace."

"Nevertheless, at the instance of his friends, he undertook the translation of some ancient Buddhist Prayers of immense religious and archeological interest."

"Great was the general astonishment. The grossest errors were combined in this work with the most palpable ignorance; in short, it was impossible to doubt of this. Not only had the dead brother alone merit, but he had also the gifts of influencing the young, for, under the dazzling action of the elder ones thought, the other had been able to reflect himself to the extent of imposing on every one."

And Yoritomo adds:

"It is unquestionable that, by throwing off the effluvia of a sound mental perception, we are able to obtain results which material efforts would achieve with more difficulty."

"Nevertheless, it is something indispensable to avail ourselves of other powerful means in order to put in vibration the forces, which surround us and must cooperate in the creation of the result, which we wish to attain."

"Every one knows that certain orders uttered during a sleep which we have brought on continue after waking in the from of an obsession, at first confused, afterward dim, but gaining in definiteness and at length tenacious, and, I should say, almost instinctive."

"The quickest and most scientific method of obtaining this sleep is the condition of torpor produced by a look, in which we have learned to embody the fascination of our influence."

"I have already mentioned the power of this look, but we shall increase it in a remarkable degree, if we can succeed in approaching the person whom we wish to influence by lightly touching his shoulders with our hands, turning the thumbs toward his neck and the fingertips on the vertebral column."

"If we are afraid to display too much the desire of influencing, and wish to avoid provoking a shrinking back, whether voluntary or not, it will be well to proceed by standing behind the person whom we wish to put to sleep and, chatting the while, place both hands on his shoulders."

"But this procedure is more difficult to put in practice, for the application of the hands must last more than a minute in order to be efficacious."

"In any case, the experiment can only succeed if it is accompanied by the putting forth of a strong and fixed power of will."

"If you give to your thought the strength and fixity required, even though the person whom you wish to put to sleep should not succumb to slumber, he would none the less become utterly subject to the mental processes which you have willed to arouse in him."

"But a single second of distraction would render all your exertions vain."

"In order to obviate this failure, it is then well to give to his thought a tangible shape and not to abandon it to a meditative condition; it must take on the features of the object of the desire, which you wish to inspire."

"For example, you desire to inculcate in some one of the love of science, make a picture representing him bending over manuscripts, or in the dim light of crypts, see him engaged attentively in deciphering inscriptions, and seeking their meaning, that veritable key of the door from which the truths of history emerge."

"If you wish to imbue him with the warlike spirit, see him confronting enemies whom he is crushing to earth."

"Similarly with every accomplishment the idea of which you wish to see born in his mind."

"At the same time, it is absolutely necessary to accentuate and to sustain the thought by words that arouse and stimulate it, by a definite enunciation of it."

"For example, you will say to the man whom you wish to render brave and resolute: 'Lift your head and accustom yourself to look danger in the face, flee not, it would pursue you and surely overtake you; but know how to measure yourself with it and confront it with a countenance unbleached with fear...'"

"It is with such words uttered in a firm voice, the while using the influence of the eye, that of the thought and that of the will, combined with the power of the fluids, that you will succeed in subjugating the most rebellious natures and in making the most inattentive ear."

"Leaders of men should never lose sight of this truth: the effort of the will produces vibratory waves the circulation of which must touch the brain of those whom they wish to subjugate."

"To allow this force the means of unbending a little, it is well, when you engage in conversation, to remain quiet while the others talk."

"While listening to each of them with attention you will avoid looking at the speaker and, without affectation, turn your eyes from his in order not to allow to be scattered the fluid which later you will send forth more efficaciously, if, instead of submitting involuntarily to the sway of the speech coming from your interlocutor, you reserve the accumulation of your psychic forces to support your discourse with all the power of occult insight."

"This must be strictly observed when it involves imposing a definite resolution, such as to deter one form a blamable action, or one contrary to that which you desire to see follow."

"Then persuasion by influence takes the form of suggestion, and, after having had recourse to the practises which we have just described, you should say to him, fixing your eyes, not on but between his, at the bridge of the nose, 'You will not do such or such a thing, because that is bad and would draw you into grievous ills'; or 'You must do such a thing, there is the solution of the problem which you seek.'"

"If the desired result should not be obtained after a first trial, you should renew it."

"It is, however, preferable to press home the conviction gradually; it thereby gains solidity, and the vacillation, so common in feeble minds, is less to be feared in proportion as the suggestion has been slow in affirmation."

The Shogun deals also with the health of the body, which, he assures us, is always related to that of the mind, and recommends means for assisting the cure of certain sick persons. Nevertheless, he advises the greatest care in the use of these agencies, however beneficent they may be.

"It is bad," he says, "roughly to compel an imaginary invalid to recognize moral error, the prime cause of physical ailments."

"We should, on the contrary, refrain from denying the existence of his sufferings and, little by little, introduce into his mind the suggestion of something better, until the moment when the idea of recovery gains possession of him."

"But in order to acquire a definite value, this idea must be the culmination of a series of other thoughts the upward gradation of which has led the patient to conceive, at first as a possibility, then as a well-grounded hope, afterward as a certainty, at last as a realization, the complete return of health definitely regained." We will not conclude this lesson on psychic influences without quoting some lines of the valuable Nippon manuscripts.

"Influence," says the author, "is synonymous with 'substitution of will'; in certain cases, the word 'creation' would be still more appropriate, for those whom we have succeeded in dominating to the extent of directing their thoughts are nearly always persons of weak character in whom the faculty of volition has remained in a rudimentary state."

"As for the others, those in whose minds we substitute our own will for that which they tend to manifest, they are generally dull or frankly vicious souls, who combine with their natural defects a kind of moral weakness, which renders them accessible to outside influence."

"When two forces come together, it is often the evil one that gives way, for, to possess the genuine endowment of influence, certain qualities must come into play which rarely fall to the lot of mediocre minds."

"The latter, totally enslaved to the satisfaction of their instincts, and their strength sapped with fleeting pleasures, lack that impassioned desire of the better, the creator of the cohesion of forces."

"The masters of conscious will alone hope to arrive at this splendid goal of influencing others, for, their spirit being imbued with nothing but the love of truth, they will ignore those passing whims that ever imprint falsehood or deceit no the thought of those who love to stray along the devious by-paths of unworthy considerations."

"The latter must never hope to possess completely the power of dominance, for they ignore the unity of thought, inasmuch as their mouth utters one word while their mind conceives another; thus the image cannot take shape in them except in an imperfect fashion, and we know how important a part that plays which we might call, in a way, the materialization of the idea in the are of influencing others."

Some pages farther on, we find the confirmation of these principles in the following lines, which adept in our modern psychology would not contradict:

"It is not given to all to possess in themselves the aggressive spirit necessary to command the influences which must emanate from our brain in order to result in forming the convictions of others; that is why it is sometimes well, instead of commanding the idea, to let it simply penetrate by itself, in order that we may arrive at its complete possession, which should not be confounded with the fact of being possessed by it."

"The difference is immense. He who possesses completely the idea, which he wishes afterward to send out from himself by the means which we have described in this chapter, in order to transmit the idea to others, is a master who commands; he who allows himself to be overcome by the obsession of an idea which takes possession of his brain and prevents his reasoning is the slave of that idea and of the acts which it will impel him to commit."

"But this cannot be, if quietly and by degrees, he allows himself to be imbued with it, for the gradual conquest implies discussion, reasoning, and even resistance, things all indispensable to the formation of rational conviction."

"Now, without conviction, influence has little weight."

"It is personal conviction, which allows us to find the words necessary to introduce it into the minds of our hearers; only personal conviction can produce adepts."

"All apostles have been persuaded of the truth of their belief, and, if some among them have been the leaders of the multitude, it is because they taught a doctrine in which they themselves sincerely believed and because their discourse spread around them the radiance of fervor, which, far better than enthusiasm, can fill men's souls and influence them."

"The gradual penetration of the idea is, therefore, to be sought in the case of those whom their natural qualities incline rather to meditation and steady adherence than to aggressive zeal."

"We might compare these different characters to those two men who, having each obtained an equal supply of wood in the forest, returned home and lit the fire to warm themselves."

"One of them let the flames mount in the beautiful spiral curves of prismatic colour, and when they died down he threw in a fresh armful, delighted with the pleasure of the sight and with the bodily comfort of the warmth."

"But soon nothing remained with which to renew the fire; the flames died away, the ruddy fire took on a vesture of gray, then a fine ash, rapidly cooling, alone remained at the bottom of the fireplace."

"The man went out again to find a fresh supply; but in passing before the hut of his friend he was astonished to see smoke arising from it, while, near the threshold, the pile of wood still lay, but little diminished."

"He went in; agreeable warmth took possession of him and he saw a modest fire gently smoldering under the ashes; all around people were standing stretching their hands for the genial sensation that pleasantly imbued them."

"So it is with gradual and continuous penetration; if it does not produce brilliant flashes, it bathes us with its beneficent suggestion, and persuaded at last that we bear within us the truth, it will be so much the easier for us to surround ourselves with all the means that the knowledge of influence places at our disposal for allowing this truth to filter gently into the minds of those who would seem to us worthy of understanding it and of spreading it in their turn."

# 7

## BY DECISION

We should not confuse the virtue of decision with that tendency which certain persons display to decide any question whatsoever without having studied it and too often without having understood it.

Like all qualities, decision is only acquired after repeated acts of reflection, determining the coordination of ideas and rendering those who devote themselves to it habitually ready to understand in a moment the advantages, at the same time as they perceive the disadvantages, of the acts which they purpose to perform.

To attain this, we must take into account all the reasons indispensable for evolving decision.

"These reasons," said Yoritomo, "are always dependent on circumstances which constantly assume a new character; for it is rarely indeed that in a man's lie the necessity for the self-same resolution makes itself felt on several occasions; even in the case in which the present emergency seems to reproduce exactly a former event, we shall find in the manner of viewing it, in the forecasting of the consequences, even in the gradual change of our feelings, a number of fine distinctions, which do not allow us to form the same opinion about it that we have in the past."

"In order to be able to discern and understand quickly to which side our decision ought to incline, in order above all to

be able to sustain it, several qualities are necessary, at the head
of which we should name:

Reflections or concentration Presence of mind
Will
Energy
Impartiality
Desire of justice Forethought

"Reflection, or rather concentration, is the faculty of self-
recollection, of shutting ourselves far away from every thought
that is not the one that should engage our attention."

"It is force that we bear within ourselves, but which we
develop to its highest degree by cultivation and application."

"It is by the habit of reflection that we succeed in reviewing
very rapidly every side of a question and in weighing the pros
and cons of the resolutions to be taken."

"This habit, when it is constant, becomes a kind of mental
gymnastics and allows us to range together in the twinkling of
an eye the reasons which militate in favour of the conclusion,
or those which should decide the abandonment of the project
which is proposed to us."

"When the balance carries it strongly to one side or the
other, the decision is plainly indicated, but many cases arise
in which the reasons in favour are quite as important and as
numerous as those against, so that the undecided man stops to
weigh them interminably."

"The man, whom the regular practice of reflection has
perfected, after having rapidly established this equilibrium, will
withdraw his mind from these motives in order to summon
others of a different order."

"He will bring in question of family, of convenience, of
surroundings; he will weight the consequences of acceptance

against the inconvenience of refusal, and he will make up his mind in a clear fashion and one devoid of any regret."

"Now comes in the second factor—Will."

"It is sometimes very hard to reply by a refusal to something, which in the midst of dangerous advantages presents seductive aspects; it is painful also to undertake certain responsibilities and to bind oneself to onerous conditions."

"But the man who is gifted with Will accepts this task with a light heart, for he knows that he is worthy of discharging it."

"However, this faculty, that admirable origin of the forces that govern life, does not always suffice to fortify decisions. It needs in order to sustain them, to call its aid Energy, which by continuousness of effort, comes to prevent the faintness, which might affect these decisions as time goes on."

"Is there a need to insist on Impartiality, the exercise of which is indispensable when considering one's innermost self?"

"The majority of the irresolute loves to deceive themselves by the delusions, which their imagination creates, and thus become only too often the architects of their own misfortune."

"Or again the decision, sometimes too sudden, is dictated to them by one reason alone, which with their tacit participation, takes on such gigantic proportions that it hides all the disadvantages, which they embellish, if they are forced to perceive them, with colours, which they know to be fictitious."

"Sincerity is also necessary with us as with others, and those who do not practice it regret sooner or later having disregarded it."

"It is from the same principle that the Desire of justice proceeds, which should predominate in all our decisions, if we wish that they brought us no remorse."

"Blundering selfishness can only dictate resolutions, which have no foundation in rectitude, for, sooner or later, regrets will arise for the acts that inevitably follow, and the concatenation of events will become the punishment of those who have neglected the laws of their neighbour."

"The principal condition of decisions that leave no bitterness behind is the foreseeing of the events, which these decisions may elicit."

"To foresee is to prevent, says an ancient maxim, and for want of foresight we often entrust ourselves to a quicksand where, in spite of every effort, we are miserably engulfed."

"We should not confound forethought with the art of divination, although, in the eyes of the vulgar, it sometimes takes on the appearance of it."

"Such persons, adepts in rational reflection, are so advanced in this science that deduction takes the place of second sight, and they succeed in formulating predictions which might pass for prophecies, if they did not themselves take care to explain in what manner they have come to form their judgement."

"It is related that an ancient Mikado, pursued by ill fortune, assembled his soothsayers in order to obtain from them the means of averting the anger of the malignant spirits."

"After much discussion, they agreed that the only means of attaining this was to build a temple consecrated to the gods of Evil, in order to appease them by paying them honour; this temple was to be built on a spot indicated by the magicians."

"However, the merciless gods demanded a preliminary sacrifice; a child was to be slain and the temple to be erected on the place crimsoned by its blood."

"After lengthy cabalistic incantations, it was decided that this child should be the first whom chance led them to meet at daybreak in the neighbouring forest."

"So the Mikado set out with the sorcerers and numerous retinues."

"The sun had just risen over the horizon, when they saw through the branches a child walking and making a way for himself through the denseness of the thicket."

"To seize him and lead him to the Mikado was the work of a moment; the poor child was immediately subjected to an examination by the magicians who all agreed I declaring that his blood would be agreeable to the evil gods, and he was committee to the men-at-arms, who dragged him after them, cruelly divulging to him what would be the tragic end of his captivity."

"Neither prayers nor supplications availed to move any of these fanatics, and the party pursued its course as far as the foot of a hill that overlooked the sea."

"Arrived at this point, the Mikado and his retinue stopped, for it had been decided to choose the flat land covering this hill for the building of the temple."

"The soldiers began to convey thither an enormous stone, which, after serving as an altar of human sacrifice was to be the foundation of the edifice."

"The child, seized with an anguish quite comprehensible, followed with attention all the preparations; but in proportion as he formed an explanation of the work of the men, his countenance cleared, an expression of hope lit up his face, and in a little while he asked permission to speak. Permission being granted him, he bowed three times before the Mikado and cried: 'O great prince, do not allow the work undertaken to proceed, for the gods of the forest are opposed to it.'"

The Mikado, who was superstitious but not wicked, looked at him sadly:

"Child," said he, "our soothsayers have decided it thus; it is the only means of appeasing the anger of the malignant spirits whose evil influences threaten the safety of the throne, it is painful to me to sacrifice so young a life, but the welfare of my empire depends on it; resign thyself and die bravely, in order to enter the realm reserved for valorous men."

"During this address, the child followed attentively the movements of the soldiers and all at once uttered a cry: 'Command them to stop, great prince, for a few steps farther and the gods of the forest will destroy them.'"

"And turning toward the densely wooded forest: 'Gods of my childhood,' he entreated, 'ye who have ever protected me, give me a fresh proof of your beneficent protection by engulfing up my tormentors together with the altar on which they would sacrifice me.'"

"Hardly had he uttered these words when, as if by magic, the soldiers who were pushing forward the heavy stone disappeared—stone and all had been drawn into the bowels of the earth by an invisible power."

"The assemblage cried out at the miracle and hastened to cut the bonds of the captive, who was lost forthwith in the depths of the forest."

"It had sufficed him, for saving his life, to remember that, when pasturing his goats, he had been stopped by quicksand, which, had it not been for his nimbleness and lightness, would have made him their prey."

"To foresee that men rolling a heavy block of stone could not avoid being swallowed up, was thus easy for him, and this child accustomed to the devices of the simple, which at every moment must protect their lives, had contracted, in the solitudes of the forests, the habit of rapid decision in all that concerns this instinct of self-preservation, so highly developed in all primitive minds."

"Threatened with immolation by men who wished to appease barbarous gods, his astuteness had forced on him the quick decision to strike awe into their minds by prophesying an event which foresight caused him to view as inevitable."

"This is the case of many soothsayers, but it is above all that of wise men, who only undertake an enterprise after they have foreseen its difficulties."

"Cells formed spontaneously as the result of change are too often produced by circumstances."

"If it is difficult to foresee their nature, it is absolutely necessary to recognize them under the vague name of bad luck and to take into account their happening, in order not to be taken by surprise when they burst upon us."

"Threatened with immolation by men who wished to appease barbarous gods, his astuteness had forced on him the quick decision to strike awe into their minds by prophesying an event which foresight caused him to view as inevitable."

"This is the case of many soothsayers, but it is above all that of wise men, who only undertake an enterprise after they have foreseen its difficulties."

"Cells formed spontaneously as the result of chance are too often produced by circumstances."

"If it is difficult to foresee their nature, it is absolutely necessary to recognize them under the vague name of bad luck and to take into account their happening, in order not to be taken by surprise when they burst upon us."

In turning over a few more pages, we come upon a definition of decision, crouched in brief and concise phraseology, such as the Nippon philosophy knows how to employ when it would sum up a thought in such a manner as to impress the mind.

"Decision," he said, "is not a spontaneous movement of the mind or of the intelligence, it is the coherent and rational choice of performing an act to the exclusion of all others which might bear a relation to the idea expressed."

"Between the moment when the reason for the decision appears and that in which it is a question of making the resolve, all the psychic states, which separate these two periods, find place."

"We have just enumerated them rapidly, but in order to grasp them in their integrity and to make them serve for the accomplishment of our projects maturely conceived and rapidly inaugurated, a kind of mental gymnastics is not unprofitable."

"For example, it is well to place us in the face of imaginary resolutions and to make up our minds while striving to do so as speedily and wisely as possible."

"It will be easy for us to measure the wisdom of our resolution, if we take as our end the events, which surround us, and if we study the delicate cases which are within reach of our knowledge."

"It is well, on seeing arise among our friends' circumstances of which we have no experience, to make use of them as a subject for our exercises and to say to ourselves:'What decision should I make if I were in his place?'"

"I do not say, mind you, that you would know all the details of the facts in such a way that it would be possible to reason from them with certainty."

"This method has the advantage of a check, for it allows you to verify the success of the decisions, which you have made in imaginary cases."

"You can thus instruct yourself in this art, so difficult and nevertheless so important, for the influence which he who is accustomed to wise and prompt decisions exerts over others is always considerable."

"Further, when some time you devote yourself to this study, you will come to make it naturally and without any effort."

"Clearness of mental vision will develop within you to such

a point that, without giving it a thought, you will come to pass a sound judgement on everything and to discern quickly what is the solution proper to each."

"Soon the fame of your wisdom will spread abroad and the weak-willed ones will come to gather around you to ask to each."

"For they are numerous who dare not venture alone in the paths of will—the creator of responsibilities." Their craven souls fear the regrets arising from a resolution of which they would have to bear the consequences, and they are like that man of whom the wise Hao-Va relates the allegorical adventure:

"A man," he said, "had to pass through a forest in order to reach a village where he hoped to meet Fortune. He set out very early in the morning and hastened to reach as quickly as possible the outskirts of the forest."

But when he had walked for some hours, he stopped and looked around him in indecision; the road laid out was long and monotonous; by taking a by—path across the wood he had perhaps a chance to shorten it... and he lost his way under the great trees.

"He walked on for an hour and found himself in a glade. He tried to get his bearings, but, not knowing what to do, he took a road by chance. He went more slowly, for he began to feel fatigue and became quite dejected, when he perceived that the road had brought him back quite near to the point whence he had set out."

"He then took the opposite road, but he could not keep count of the windings that it made, so that after a long course he saw the glade again."

"That was for him the moment of a great resolution, he gave up definitely the side roads and set out on the first road, which he had followed and which led directly to the village."

"But the sun set behind the trees; night covered the forest

with its veil, and the distracted man was obliged to interrupt his journey, now useless, for Fortune had failed to wait for him."

"Do not laugh at this man," cried the Shogun, "you are for the most part like him; you wander in the labyrinths of indecision instead of following the way pointed out by the will; you lose your presence of mind at the first objection; you avoid being sincere with yourselves by avowing that you heedlessly lose your way in unknown roads, and when at length you pause before a definite course, opportunity has wearied of waiting for you."

"Despise these irresolute ones, you who aspire to become those whose influence radiates over the souls of others."

"Be counsellors with well-weighed and prompt decisions; do not stray in the by-paths of which you do not know the windings, and learn to become safe and enlightened guides for yourselves before pointing out the way to those of whom your influence has made attentive and devoted disciples."

It seems that to add any comment to these teachings would be to risk weakening them, for these appeals burning with energy, as well as the luminous illustrations that accompany them, can serve as a rule of conduct for the people of this day as well as for the far distant disciples of Yoritomo.

# 8

## BY RATIONAL AMBITION

"Ambition is accessible only to the brave; they alone can discover the treasure hidden within it, by breaking up the sham gems of illusion and intrigue."

These words of Yoritomo should be known to all those who set out for the conquest of life. They should be inscribed in letters of gold on the frontals of schools where the young make their initial start, which, in most cases, decides their future.

"Ambition," again says the old philosopher, "should, equally with goodness or any other virtue, form the object of rational teaching."

"But for that it would be necessary to disengage ourselves from prejudices, which brand it as a fault, which we ought to dissemble."

"He is an ambitious one," say the vulgar, "when they wish to discredit the achievements of a man whose aspirations raise him above the commonplace things of life."

"They do not dream that, in order to form a genuine and productive ambitious man, it is necessary to possess a great number of qualities which people who pride themselves on their modesty will always ignore."

"What is understood generally by modesty?"

"Is it the shrewd reserve of any ambitious man who fears to display his appetites in order not to be liable to restrain them before having found the means of satisfying them?"

"Is it not too often the sham virtue, which under the borrowed lineaments of humility hides the terrible defect of weakness?"

"Would it not rather be the tinsel in which idleness likes to dress itself up in order to abandon itself with ease to its favourite vice?"

"Modesty can serve as a standard for all the vices, which we have just mentioned; it is the enemy of courageous undertakings, of acts that require a display of energy that ambition or boldness alone can decide on."

"It is besides nearly always the sign of a want of confidence in oneself. It is again the safeguard of the self-respect of the incapable."

"Many weak mortals, irresolute, idle, or incompetent, instead of seeking to acquire the qualities which they lack, prefer to declare loudly: 'Oh, as for me, I shall never succeed in attaining this end, for the good reason that I shall not undertake it. I am a modest person, I am. I have a hatred of fame and renown surrounding my name; I desire only obscurity, and I pity keenly all those who are tormented by a desire to shine!'"

"They say all this without thinking that the first condition of the being of modesty consists in ignorance of its existence."

"He who prides himself on modesty will never be a modest man, for the moment he sets out to establish his virtue he acts like a braggart."

"If he is really convinced of his unimportance, if the diffidence of himself which he has is sincere, we should pity him very keenly, for he will suffer in feeling himself so insignificant, and this feeling will lead him, little by little, to hypochondria unless he inclines to the side of jealousy."

"Such is almost without exception the punishment of the weak; they have not themselves courage to undertake great things and they do not forgive those who achieve them."

"There is, however, a kind of modesty before which we ought to bow; it is that of the learned man who, finding his happiness in the quest of knowledge and truth, makes no attempt to gain glory, and waits in the midst of his apparatus and his parchments for it to come to him, while preparing himself to welcome it with no more emotion than an ordinary visitant."

"This sentiment would be worthy of admiration if it were not so often mingled with an inveterate selfishness, behind which is hidden an indifference toward others, carried to the point of excluding anxiety to cause others to share in the benefit of ones discoveries."

"This kind of modest man who ignores thus his duty toward others is less useful to humanity than an ambitious man, who, eager to increase his fame, will make known the result of his work to the sound of the trumpet."

"For, in order to be fruitful, everything in our life must bear relation to others."

"It is by developing ambition in their breasts that the leaders of the multitude have succeeded first in gaining a hearing and then in carrying conviction."

"What generous impulse can we expect from a man who has only one desire; to shut himself up in the selfish quiet of a life the works of which he jealously keeps to himself?"

These facts, already true enough in the days of Shogun, assume a fresh significance in our time, when they might become the textbook of those whom we designate by the name of those who have arrived and who are in the majority of cases nothing if not ambitious ones—I was almost going to say the rightfully ambitious.

And why? Ambition, when it excludes unworthy means and spurns intrigue, is it not one of the noblest passions that could be conceived?

National ambition furnishes our projects with wings, which allow them to mount above commonplace ideas; it is thanks to ambition that we experience emulation, which carries us along the Better way. Without ambition should we have knowledge of those marvelous discoveries, which make our age that of progress par excellence? And it might be said that Yoritomo set forth the splendid incentives given to the ambitious of our time by benefactors keen beyond measure on improvement, when he says:

"It is a crime to destroy in the breasts of children, under the pretense of modesty, that self-confidence which should shine like a star in the hearts of all."

"It would be more useful, on the contrary, to found rewards for distribution to those who, with a noble end in view, devote themselves to undertakings sometimes called rash."

"Such are the veritable handmaids of destiny, since, by their desire for the better, they sometimes succeed n discovering an improvement, which ameliorates the lot of other men."

"Besides, it is well that every effort should be rewarded by an increase in the possessions of the man who has made the attempt and who, by his special qualifications, has promoted a success the good results of which are never limited to him."

"Justice demands that inventors should derive profit from their inventions, this will allow them to devote more of their time to the pursuit of another discovery."

It will perhaps be objected that there are some ambitious men who produce nothing. That whose success profits only themselves and who cannot spread around them joy that arises from generous benefactions. The world is certainly populated with a large number of selfish persons and it will assuredly be difficult to prevent this state of things, but it would be a serious mistake to believe that these people are altogether useless.

Ambition is never without the great desire of attaining everything which gratifies it, and what better means is there of proclaiming its success than to command a large retinue, to give banquets, and to build palaces, or plant spacious gardens.

Even granting that the ambitious man who has attained satisfaction is hard-hearted and neglects works of charity, do not the workmen who labour in providing the trappings of his vanity profit largely by an ambition, which procures for them the means of subsistence.

By the law of human evolution, the money obtained by the ambitious will come of necessity to ameliorate the condition of the humble, in the same way as their works and their discoveries will always succeed in increasing the fund of public knowledge, for only the modest man is able to keep to himself the result of his labours.

He who would master fame or fortune, on the other hand, hastens to make public the most trifling success; true, he sometimes exaggerates it, but the fault is not his alone; it may be imputed to the habit of disparaging those on whom Fortune seems to smile.

"I heard one day," said the Shogun, "a man whom I knew to be of a serious turn of mind relate that he had spent three years in completing a work."

"Now I had followed his studies with interest, and I knew that this task had required of him in all a hundred and fifty days."

"I was, therefore, astonished, and questioned him on the reasons of a falsehood, which puzzled me the more that I knew his habitual truthfulness."

"Child," replied he, "do you not understand that if I were to admit spending so little time in perfecting my work people would not fail to find it incomplete or too lightly thought out? It is not sufficient to be capable; we must not shock any one in proving overmuch this capability. For this assertion of a quality, which they do not possess, causes suffering in the envious who do not fail to revenge themselves for it by belittling it to others. It is their method of succeeding in placing themselves in the same class; unable to rise it to the level of people of merit, they try to bring the latter down to their level."

The ambitious man escapes these cheap devices; he is from the first too full of his projects to give time to insignificant jealousies.

In short, he rarely resents the sentiment of envy, for he is always convinced that he will succeed in surpassing the success of those who are competing for the same goal as him.

Moreover, ambition is a sure and swift means of influence. This is, in the first place, because men have always a tendency to follow the man who draws them in the direction of light and progress.

Again, because it is almost always from the following of the ambitious, that those are chosen to attain honours and fortune.

It forms no part of the program of the successful ones to drag after them the incapable or weak; this is why their influence over their pupils extends the more in proportion as the latter imitate and follow them. For the ambitious man is not displeased to raise himself near to him one who will step into his vacant place when he shall have advanced some degrees further.

And here is one of the primary reasons for the influence which rational ambition can exert on the men's minds. The lure of gain or distinction binds men to train of him who is in a position to give such a way to them.

It is in his power to be able to employ this influence profitably for disseminating good and the love of the Better around him; it is in his power to instill into the hearts of his devotees aspirations toward a noble end; it is in his power always to put them on their guard against intrigues which would have the effect of diminishing the beauty of their ambition.

There is between the ambitious man and the intriguer all the difference that separates beauty from ugliness. The first proceeds, with head erect, toward a definite goal that he has long and maturely decided to choose; he disdains paltry methods; he seeks only to attain the end that he has set before himself. He goes, without concerning himself with the stones on the road, his heart full of confidence, sustained by faith in his star, which he never loses from view, notwithstanding the clouds that hide it from time to time. He lifts his eyes too high to recognize the vulgar herd of the envious who swarm around his feet, he is content to spurn them with the tip of his shoe; unless, overmuch beset or tormented by their incessant attacks, he crushes them under foot, as we do with an importunate insect, which we try at first to drive away and which we destroy, without ill feeling, simply to rid ourselves of its repeated and irritating stings.

The intriguer, on the other hand, rarely raises himself above the horde or mean desires and paltry jealousies. Unlike the ambitious man, he acts with no other end in view than the procuring for himself of money or pleasure.

No lofty thought ever enters his head longer than the time necessary to turn it to account, while he considers it only under its mercenary aspect, and this accomplished, he passes to a class of ideas the burdens of which is never the same.

The desire of distinction never haunts the dreams of the intriguer; he reduces everything to the narrowness of his aspirations and entertains no project that does not lend itself to his base sentiments. Is that to say that we should despise money and seek after poverty?

"Not so," said Yoritomo, "for the poor man exercises little influence over the multitude. Again, most achievements demand considerable application and loss of time, and we could not lavish it in this way if we were obliged to take thought for the earning of our daily bread."

"It is, therefore, well to find resources which will allow the pursuit of an end without being compelled to give it up in order to provide for the necessities of daily life, and which will also save us from compromises of conscience which the greatest leaders of men must sometimes endure, when they do not possess that advantage, indispensable to him who does not wish to diverge from his course: assurance as to the primary needs of life."

"This should be the first aim of the man who wishes to win honour, fortune, or distinction. Before rushing forth on toilsome paths on the chance of meeting such, we should be sure of the possibility of pursuing them and not risk missing them because the necessity of providing for our daily wants compels us to pause just when we had hoped to attain them."

We cannot but admire once again the wisdom of Yoritomo, who once more is found in agreement with the greatest thinkers.

Theognis said: "The man who is broken down by poverty can neither speak nor act; his tongue is tied and his feet are chained."

It is only too true; downright poverty is a disadvantage, for it often compels those who suffer to pay court to the fortunate ones of this world. In any case, it is a hindrance to all undertakings, which require sustained effort and peace of mind, which can only be obtained by those certain of the morrow.

But, you will say, everybody cannot be rich, and many, becoming so, have known poverty; is it not then an insuperable obstacle?

"Poverty," he said, "is a hindrance only if it consists in absolute want, and in this case it is usually the result of idleness or of mismanagement of our affairs."

"We should not reckon as poor the man who earns a scanty livelihood but whose peace of mind cannot be changed by the suffering resulting from the lack of necessaries."

"Such a one can, when he has fulfilled the duties of his station in life, devote himself to the aspirations of a lawful ambition."

"Rarely does he enjoy independence, for in order to live he has to accept many humiliations or spend a considerable portion of his time in quests which have as their object the insurance of his livelihood."

"If he is sincere in these efforts, he will not long remain poor, for he will soon find employment, no matter what, and if he is endowed with ambition he will quickly succeed in distinguishing himself in it."

"From that time, poverty will be for him nothing but a specter of the past, for he will work to better his position and he will soon become one to be envied. Poverty is only allowable if it is voluntary, which is to say, if it is the result of a decision, which prefers that condition to another more brilliant but less independent. Nevertheless, riches are the key of many marvels and they are above all the key of many influences."

"Not only is the man of great possessions in a better position to make those whom he patronizes listen to his words, but the prestige of his success surrounds him with a halo of influence, which if he is wise, he will use to better the lot of his neighbour."

"We do not receive kindness from an empty hand; we have nothing to expect from a man tormented by care for the morrow. What words can fall from a mouth sealed by hunger?"

It is true that fortune, considered simply from the point of view of riches, is not an exalted ideal, but we must nevertheless welcome it as the consecration of success and as a power of which the wise man knows how to dispose for the good of his fellows.

It is a means of exciting interest and of influencing the

multitude, for the people will always be disposed to listen to the advice of a man who has had the ability to acquire great possessions.

It is then in the power of the man who has been able to acquire this power of money to make use of it for establishing his beneficent influence over the minds of those who are disposed to trust in him.

After his other successes, this last will not be a matter of indifference to the man who, while monopolizing the empire of the purse, will be proud to endeavor after the authority of the empire of the mind.

Thanks to the prestige which his riches confer on him he will be able to spread the rays of influence as far as the boundaries of the attraction of thought, and as it displays itself above all in action he will gather around him a band of brave and intelligent men, ready to imitate him in spreading abroad the ideas which he ahs inculcated in them and to speak as he has taught them.

"Do not wait for the desired object to come to you, but rise up and set out to look for it; when you have found it you will undertake its conquest, and when it becomes your possession you will gather together your friends to make them share in your good fortune and to tell them by what means it has befallen you." In acting thus, he will follow the teaching of Yoritomo who said:

"Ambition is a gate opening on magnificent gardens, but the fortunate ones who have entered it should not pause there; they will pass beyond the entrance in order to survey the road and to make a sign to passers-by, pointing out to them the way."

And this profound psychologist adds:

"A discovery brings no real joy to its finder until he can announce it, and we should rejoice at this almost universal law, for it is the cause of an improvement evolved by ambition, the happy influence of which awakens the instinct of conquest dormant in the breast of every man worthy of the name."

# 9

## BY PERSERVERANCE

Persuasion, like good example, perseverance is among, if not the most brilliant, at least the most active agents of influence. It is a faculty borne within them by men conscious of their power, those who, by virtue of faith in their own merit, advance to achievement with that confidence which gives birth to all notable successes and all productive achievements.

Perseverance is the triumph of willpower over the weakness of the will; it is the result of a profound study of the determining causes, the combination of which is bound to end in success; it is, in short, the slow but sure ascent toward a goal that assumes a more definite shape the nearer we approach it.

Few persons are born with a silver spoon in their mouths, but everybody can aim at conquering fortune by a series of continual and rational efforts.

The man who would spring up thirty cubits at a single leap would spend his life in ridiculous attempts, but if he wishes steadily to mount the steps that lead him to that height, he will attain it, sooner or later according to the dexterity, the agility, and the perseverance that he displays.

The steps, it is true, are often made of shaky stones. They have gaps between them that make one dizzy, where they are so uncertain that it is difficult to keep a foothold on them.

This is the point where those who possess the virtue of perseverance make themselves known; by their unshakable will they can ward off every danger; they balance themselves on the shaky stones almost on tiptoe and advance onto the next step; they feel fascinated by the giddy depths beneath them quickly they raise their heads, they proceed gazing on their star and they guard themselves against possible slips by making sure of one foot before lifting the other from the ground.

"For perseverance is the mother of many gifts; from her is born circumspection which clasps hands with application and patience. It is incredible to what degree the man who is gifted with patience is proof against the pitfalls of Fate; hope and cheerfulness are two unanswerable arguments under most circumstances; application comes to hold up their hands, and few undertakings can resist their combined influence."

"It is related that the great scholar Yuan-Shi, plagued by the sour temper of his wife who was jealous of his knowledge, could find no way of working at home, for this termagant went so far as to throw his manuscripts about and burn the sheets of vellum on which he set down his thoughts."

"He therefore resolved, when he was at home to divide his time between gardening and contemplation. But from the time that he got into the palanquin which conveyed him daily from his country house to the town where he was employed, he recouped himself for his enforced inactivity; in this way he produced, after some months, a work of great value, which was universally commended and admired."

"News of this reached his wife, who asked him astonishingly how he found the time to write, considering that outside his professorship he was not engaged in any intellectual occupation."

"Yuan-Shi was a simple soul; he related to her how he had managed to reconcile his work with her unreasonableness. She was so affected by this proof of his desire not to annoy her and so impressed by the calm and indomitable will of her husband that from that day she ceased to forbid him to engage in work which brought him distinction and shed its rays upon her in the form of caresses that saved her wifely self-respect."

Our modern civilization boasts many examples of this assiduous application: Doctor Good translated Lucréce while visiting his patients; he had in his carriage all the material necessary for the translation of the book and in this way he made use of the minutes between each visit.

Doctor Darwin did the same; he wrote his notes while going his rounds, and upon returning home, he had only to classify them.

One may also mention a man named White, who was employed in a law office, who learned Greek while journeying from the office to his home. We know the instance of Aguesseau who employed the time that elapsed between the announcement of meals and the moment when the company took their places at the table to write an excellent book, which he smilingly presented to his wife as a practical lesson in method and perseverance. History is rich in similar anecdotes and this proves incontestably that saying of Bossuet:

"A little suffices for each day, if each day acquires a little."

Do we reckon what might be the production of one hour a day won from frivolous pursuits to which we give so many drops of our life fallen into the gulf of eternity?

"He," said the Shogun, "who should cut down a branch every day would end by clearing a way through the densest forest."

He adds judiciously:

"But he should not think of going back, for the branches grow again and he would find the way closed." That is to say that perseverance must never slacken; return is not allowed to those who should widen the road for their disciples to follow and we cannot repeat too often: It is by the power of personal effort and of application that the most brilliant and solid reputations are slowly formed.

"Experience," says G.A. Mann, "tells us that we must have, in order to succeed, method in everything that we do and also perseverance; if we do not possess these two qualities we should develop them, and that by thinking constantly of them and by contemplating the idea which represents them."

"Persevere then! To what end do you say? Simply because by persevering you form your will, besides have the chance of attaining your end."

"Persevere like a brute! Not at all. It is necessary, that in continuing what you have begun, your will, your intelligence, your sensibilities be ever on the alert."

"It is this unceasing activity in yourself that is the reward of your effort. The road on which you walk may, perhaps, not lead you where you wished to go. But probably it will lead you to a better place. And for your walk you will become a good walker, which will be certainly due to the impulse, which you needed to be able to attain the goal, that is to say, success. Will without perseverance and without method could not exit."

Perseverance admits of a combination of active qualities and of virtues that might be called passive, for they demand no apparent effort. Nevertheless, they are more rare than one might think, for they are not often the endowment of weak minds.

The latter can only with difficulty concentrate themselves on a task that requires a little application; they are the slaves of the instability of their impressions; beginnings, however arduous, always find them full of enthusiasm, but his fervor soon grows cold, and if success does not present itself immediately, they will hasten to give up their project and devote themselves to another which will soon have a like ending. Unremitting action can also be reckoned in a number of these virtues, passive indeed but indispensable, of which we have just spoken. The practice of bending the will to listen to some purpose is sometimes a talent of a high order, for it is one of the best means of winning the sympathies of those who are speaking with us.

"I hate," said Yoritomo, "the sort of people who let their thoughts wander blindly instead of seeking to glean profit from what they hear. Nothing is more disconcerting than to feel the attention of one to whom one is speaking to drifting away and wandering after his thoughts, while you would like to convince him by your words."

"This lack of attention is always the mark of a vacillating will which cannot bring itself to follow an idea by concentrating its mental powers or an examination of the various aspects which it presents."

"When dealing with inferiors, this frivolous inattention may pass as a sign of contempt; besides, it is always in opposition to the influence which we might exercise over them."

"What should we think of a chief whom a poor man comes to consult and who instead of listening to him kindly, should busy himself as I have known them, in giving orders to his servants and arranging the hanging of his house and should let his musicians go on playing?"

"The unfortunate man would go out of the Lord's house with the bad impression, and if ever he had to seek help or advice he would take care or not betake himself a second time to the man who treated his request with steady disdain."

"Influence over others is acquired especially by perseverance of the will and concentration of thought, the undulations of which, projected around us come to reach the minds which we wish to impress."

And, entering once more into the domain of psychology, the Shogun speaks to us of this fascinating mystery of the contagion of thought, which according to have as a primary cause of influence and cannot fail by perseverance determination to produce it:

"There is no doubt," he said, "that thought is a contagious factor of influence, good or bad."

"Who has not had occasion to remark this in the case of fear?"

"In an assemblance composed of the bravest people that it is possible to meet, taken individually, one man stricken with fear or, if he can express his feelings in a forcible manner, will succeed in imparting to each of the rest, in different degrees it may be, the disquietude and uneasiness which he experiences."

"There are a few doughty warriors who at the recital of something concerning the mysteries of the world beyond have not felt a slight shiver, which the site of wholesale carnage, together with the consciousness of the gravest perils, could not have caused them to experience."

"This phenomenon, caused by the irradiation of thought, is an undeniable proof of the influence which it can exercise, for not only is it possible to penetrate the minds touched by the undulations of our own thought, but the thought of others, elicited by ourselves, comes back to us on the same undulations that are spread out from our brain."

"This is why we often see one who wished to shed fear or around him feel that same fear by receiving the waves of thought that he has produced in his audience."

"It is the same with laughter. Very few are they who can resist the infection of a burst of laughter; even with those least inclined to merriment laughter is infectious in a high degree; for at first involuntary, in a way mechanical, it ends by becoming natural, so that, at the moment it breaks out, the simplest expression, the most sedate words assumes in the imagination so comical an aspect that merriment increases to the point of not being able to utter them without provoking a fresh outburst."

"But what happens if the next day we wish to relate to this incident?"

"No longer submitted to the attractive influence of the thought of others, no longer receiving from them the undulations, the vibrations of which had reached us on the previous day, our state of mind is completely different, we perceive the inanity (sometimes we should say the foolishness) of what had amused us so highly on the preceding day, and no longer laughingover it ourselves it is impossible for us to entertain others with it."

"On the other hand, if the storyteller—either of set purpose or spontaneously—begins by laughing himself at the remembrance of what he is about to relate, it is seldom that this merriment, if it appears genuine, does not spread to others, who will laugh at first by infection, afterward of necessity, because merriment is the pervading thought."

"What we have just said on the subject of fear or of laughter applies to everything else."

"With perseverance, you succeed in causing effectively to penetrate the minds of your hearers the thoughts the emission of which will attract similar thoughts, and their undulations returning to affect you will increase your conviction, giving you the us the more power to spread its around you."

It is from this standpoint that the Shogun sets out to oppose the emission of evil thoughts:

"It is," said he, "a weapon which always recoils on the man who would make use of it."

"The evil thought traverses the same cycle as the other and returns to us strengthened with hatred for others."

"What can we expect from those whose minds we cause to germinate wickedness and the desire of evil? As soon as they believe themselves capable, it is against us first of all of that they will seek to exert themselves, and they will do it involuntarily by bringing back to us our thought, magnified and disfigured, so that we shall endure it without recognizing it."

"You see why perseverance should only be applied to the gaining of good, and as soon as we think we have come into association with it, it will be our duty to inculcate its principles into those who, living around us, are subjected to our influence."

"But we must not limit our efforts to this; we must aim farther and higher; it will not suffice to initiate them into good things, we must also give them the taste to cultivate them, and to that end arouse in them the desire of perseverance, which makes possible the most difficult undertakings and gives us a power that we cannot limit."

"Like some steel implement, the drop of water perforates the rock, wears a way the hardest stone, and without slacking, pursues this work which the implement would have begun more successfully perhaps, but the breaking or wearing out of the tool would have interrupted, perforce, the work which the eternal drop of water accomplishes by the tenacity and perseverance of its action."

"Do not then seek to force slow-moving minds, but surround them, penetrate them by your perseverance and its influence, sometimes obscure but always certain, will spread itself abroad in beneficent undulations, the continuance of which will create a power."

# 10

## BY THE PRESTIGE GAINED
## FROM CONCENTRATION

Concentration is one of the most marvelous forces that can be conceived. Without concentration, no success is possible; if it is present, we must consider it as the work of chance, not reckon too much on its duration, and remember that the popular proverb which says:

"He who comes to the sound of the flute goes back to the sound of the drum."

In other words, what a chance circumstance has brought may depart on the wings of an unforeseen happening. Far different is the success which we acquire by reason, that having sought it and willed it with all our powers, we have strained every effort to evoke it and no longer hug it to ourselves for fear or that it should leave us.

Fidelity to an idea is always the initial step to all successes. For if an idea has no time to become at home with us, if what is rightly called the crystallization of thought does not form the foundation of every decision, we shall find it impossible to give it definite shape, and it will fade away like impalpable smoke. If, on the other hand, we know how to exercise concentration, this idea will soon become a focus of organization around which the association of ideas will come to marshal the reasons that determined the action, which we have in mind.

"Thoughts are things," said Prentice Mulford. Without wishing to follow him in his abstruse explanation of the statement, it is easy to imagine how true the saying is, seeing that in thinking deeply on a subject we succeed in picturing it to ourselves in an almost tangible fashion."

"There is no doubt," said Yoritomo, "that concentration develops all our senses and brings them to a degree of remarkable acuteness."

"It stands to us in the stead of knowledge, for by its means we acquire the facility, that is to say the gift, of realizing readily and easily the things of which we have formed a conception. There is no work, even manual, that concentration does not lighten for us."

"If a man has to lift a heavy mass, do you think that he will do it as well if he is occupied with some other thought as if he said simply and solely:' I wish to lift this mass."

"Then his nerves are at tension, all his faculties bend themselves to the act with a force necessary to perform it; his brain strives after the means to assist the physical effort, for the muscles are the slaves of the will; he, therefore, who succeeds in concentrating himself on a manual labour is certain to perform it with a minimum of fatigue, for he will be able to husband his strength, he will save himself from dissipating them in useless exertions, and he will concentrate all his faculties of attention, of calculation, of ingenuity, and of muscular power in order to succeed."

"This is how so many jugglers achieve perfection in their art; by concentration they have reached such a point of self absorption therefore them nothing exists outside their own particular performance."

"But if one day they, in a fit of passion, allow their thoughts to wander toward the object of their anger or of their love, they find that they are no longer themselves; their actions become less sure, the make bungles and end by being unable to regain their nerve, except with a violent effort that drives away the fancy and allows them to recall their thoughts to the one point where they should keep them."

"To think of the act which we are performing, to think of it alone, to concentrate everything and forget everything outside of it, there is the secret of so many successes, the explanation of so many good fortunes, that also of the immense influence which certain men exert over their fellows."

"We must," said the Shogun, "be able to concentrate ourselves on one act at a time and to force our attention to the fullest degree to the manner in which we can attract others to imitate us. We are the shapers of our destiny, and we should aspire to become those of the destiny of others."

"To gain this end, nothing should appear insignificant to us, and if we think sensibly we shall see that everyone of our acts, however commonplace it may seem to us, is, if it is performed with the desire of good, a step toward a realization, sometimes imposing the fate of which, however, depends on a series of similar acts, equally paltry taken separately, but the essential for the adequacy of one of them might mar the perfection of the whole, if not jeopardize success altogether."

And in his flowery language the shogun adds:

"What is one link more or less in the chain several meters long? So trifling a thing that its absence would not be noticed. Nevertheless, if this link is badly riveted, this insignificant detail will suffice to break the chain."

"Every work is made up of a chain of acts more or less infinitesimal; the perfection of each of them contributes to that of the whole and sometimes suffices or a slight slackness in the performance of one of these acts to jeopardize the success of the undertaking."

In fact, which of us has not had to regret negligence, which has come to hinder the success of a project? In our age of electricity and of strenuous life, these remarks are still more true been they would be at any other time. Does it not happen every day they missed train causes us the loss of the benefit of some business, which because of the delay escapes us?

Now, if we wish to be perfectly sincere with ourselves, we shall admit that on most occasions this delay is to only to our own carelessness; we were too late for meals, or we wasted time on talk, which would have been quite easy for us to curtail.

All the trouble arose from want of concentration, which allowed us to lose sight of the one thing that should have been for us of the utmost importance. If we will reflect well on it, we shall see them most of our troubles can be set down to carelessness. Take, if you wish, the case, which we have just mentioned: A missed train prevents the settlement of the important business.

Thoughtless people will get out of this by saying: "I have not had a chance"; others those who thoughts are directed by a mastermind, which is an adept at concentration, will recollect themselves, will mentally review all the passing events of the day, and will thereby conclude that they are responsible for that happening so deplorable for their interests.

What can or should they do? Simply devote themselves to one of the exercises most recommended by thinkers; concentrate their faculties on the principal act of the day which was the settlement of the business which called them out, and, once well persuaded of its importance, suit all their acts to it.

They would thus have avoided losing a few minutes or the hour which caused them to fail, for, filled with their determination, they would have cut short any business that it was not indispensable to conclude, or cut off some moments from talk the continuance of which was less important for them than the journey which they had to make.

"Each day," said Yoritomo, "brings with it a round of duties of unequal importance; we must know how to distinguish that which should take precedence, and subordinate to it our mode of life for that day."

"Everything that we do should bear a relation to it; even if certain things should seem mutually exclusive, we must avoid them, inasmuch as they form part of the whole of those things which go to make up realization. By being willing to sacrifice nothing we succeed too often in accomplishing nothing."

"We know the story of the man who one day found two robbers in his garden and set out to pursue them. He ran after them at first for a time, then at a fork in the road one of the two turned off to the right, while the other pursued his way. The man, undecided for a moment, rushed down the byroad, saying to himself that he would catch more easily the one that took the hard road, but after a time, out of breath he perceived that he was not as quick as the robber, and bethought himself that the other was bigger and stouter and on that account easier to overtake."

"He, therefore, retraced his steps and rushed along the main road; but the man whom he was pursuing had had the time, in spite of his want of agility, to gain ground, and the pursuer puffed and blew in vain. He soon had the mortifications of seeing him disappear, and his neighbours made fun of him."

How many times do we act likewise, without perceiving it, when we pursue two different ends and give them up, first one, of then the other, according to the inclination of our idleness or of our whims? This fault to will never be committed by those who practice concentration. They will never risk making themselves a laughingstock like the men of whom Yoritomo speaks, for they will set out in pursuit of an undertaking only after reflecting deeply on the possibilities of success, and they will take every precaution against giving it up before they have brought it to a successful issue.

They who would be adequately prepared for this kind of reflection ought to bring themselves to it by the habitual contemplation of a thought. It is well to maintain the attention on the alert, and to keep oneself from every distraction by the repetition of one or several sayings the bearing a relation to this thought, giving it concrete and definite form and persuading us of the necessity of concentration.

Other methods also are employed with success; they've made up those exercises, which should be practiced by all those who wish to acquire any science, whatever it may be. Of these methods, several were already known in the time of Yoritomo, and it is she who recommends us that called "of the collar":

"Have," said he, "a collar containing about 200 beads of jade or of any other stone, if your means do not allow you to make use of jewels; take care to string them not too close together in order to be able to take them off easily and make them slide slowly one over the other, counting ten between each bead."

"Your mind during this time should be occupied with only one thing:to allow between the beads the same space of time, that is to say, not to say the numbers too fast or too slowly, and to it in such a way, all the time that this exercise lasts, as to think thus regularly of nothing but GOOD."

"When you find it impossible to keep up your thought, revive it as soon as you can and begin again. At first, it will be well not to extend the experiment farther than five or six beads. Afterward you can increase it, and some thinkers are mentioned who had such a mastery over their imagination that they went right to the end of the beads without slackening."

With the same collar the Shogun shows us yet another exercise.

"You will take off," said he, "a handful of the beads (without counting them), in such a way that you are ignorant of the exact number, and, having fastened the collar together again, letting the place of joining be in sight, which will serve as a starting point, you will count aloud each bead that you take off with your fingertip."

"That done, you will begin again three times; if you find the same number each time it means that your power of concentration has been sufficient to keep your attention without letting it wander."

"Where you find a different number, you should begin again until you obtain the same result three times a succession."

We might smile at the simplicity of these methods, nevertheless those who are devoted adepts in concentration know how difficult these results are to realize, if they wish to be sincere with themselves; before obtaining the same count of beads three times, they must often begin the experiment over again twenty times, for thought escapes easily when one can no longer keep it in subjection.

The Shogun recommends us yet other exercises:

"Sit down," said he, "comfortably on a seat soft enough to prevent your feeling any discomfort; this is very essential, for the least physical discomfort distracts the attention by directing it is to the feeling of uneasiness which you experience."

"That done you will rest your hands on your breast, the palms well open, the fingers spread out."

"The left hand will be placed near the girdle and the other near the throat; you will slowly pass the left hand down to the waist while you will slowly pass the left-handed down to the waist while you lift the other as far as the neck, taking great care, when the two hands meet, to touch lightly the tip of the middle finger of the left hand with the tip of the middle finger of the right hand."

"During the few minutes that this exercise lasts, you will do it in such a way as to think of nothing except the care of letting the fingers touch one another toward the middle of the breast, and in consequence of accelerating for retarding the movement in order to arrive at this result."

"During all this time force yourself to think of nothing else."

This is what our modern philosophers recommend us to the name of "de-vitalization." De-vitalization is the act of shutting oneself out from external impressions and moral sensations; if it is a kind of arrest of thought, or rather of rupture of thought, which one concentrates on something so plainly commonplace that it gives birth to a sensible rest for us.

This is the first step that leads to one of the most satisfactory forms of concentration: isolation. Without isolation, no meditation is possible, and consequently there is great difficulty in concentration. Now we have just seen what part this faculty plays in training the mind. It is that which allows us to rally our scattered physical powers and to unite them on the same point, localizing them alone on the phases of the subject that engages our attention.

Atkinson recommends us to devote ourselves to the study of any object whatsoever and to force ourselves to limit the effort of our thoughts to that object alone. But this meditation may form the excuse for many mental vagaries. He advises us to take a piece of paper and to concentrate our attention solely on the thought of this scrap; but is not this on the other hand a dangerous excuse for fancy to come into play? Contemplate it: this piece of paper once formed part of some material. What material? Was it the white muslin of bridal veils? Was it, on the other hand, the flimsy fabric in which a courtesan arrays herself? Whose hands tore it? In what religious processions or in what wretched dens was it used?

Later, by what changes did it come to this condition of a scrap of paper? The imagination takes fire afresh. We conjure up the atmosphere of a factory, we think of the processes of manufacture, etc. You see that we are already far removed from concentration. Doubtless, Yoritomo also believes this when he says:

"If you wish to devote yourself sincerely to the practice of concentration, guard yourself against allowing your thoughts to wander from the corolla to the stalk of the flower."

This means the one object alone, and that strictly limited, should engage our attention if we wish to succeed in controlling our attention to the point at which it responds to our first call like an obedient servant. Many feather—brained people think it a good excuse when they say:

"It is not my fault, I forgot."

Not suspecting that forgetfulness is itself the fault with which they do not wish to be charged. It is an excuse glibly assigned by those whose moral infirmity is so evident that they are unable on their own accounts to make any effort worth the while. It is the excuse of the weak and of people lacking courage. It is a certificate of physical incapacity awarded to those who have not in them the energy to practise self-recollection.

Meditation, which is closely allied to concentration, is the state of inward contemplation, which allows us to shut ourselves in from external things so as to engage our thoughts solely on the subject, which we have set before ourselves. The difference between meditation and concentration lies in the greater freedom allowed to thought in the former state.

"Meditation," said Yoritomo, "is like a target of which concentration is the bullseye. Every arrow which hits the target has certainly attained its end, but those which quiver at its centre are the only ones which, in case of defense, would have sufficed to make our enemy bite the dust."

And he adds:

"Meditation is valuable above all because it is a rest; it is a kind of mental anesthesia which allow for us to have faith in our liberty of thought, even when, nevertheless, we still confine it but less closely than in concentration."

"We could not devote ourselves to a fruitful meditation without being prepared for it by self-absorption. We must then allow ourselves to be slowly permeated by the idea which we wish to fathom and all the influences of which we wish to receive its."

"But we ought to fear one redoubtable enemy—distraction. Nothing is more difficult for those who do not habitually practice this lesson than to meditate successfully, without letting the thoughts wander after ideas which are connected with one another but which end, by reason of their number and diversity, by being completely removed from the initial point."

In fact, we have all experienced the impression of which the Shogun speaks; it has happened to all of us, after long periods of reflection, to find ourselves a hundred leagues from the subject which we desired to conjure up, and when we wish to take account of the road traversed we find ourselves altogether amazed at the imperceptible concatenation of thoughts, which, without seeming to be foreign to the subject of our meditation, have drawn us in the direction of ideas completely dissimilar.

This is one of the familiar phases of distraction, the foe of concentration. This is why Yoritomo puts us on our guard against meditation, of which the dreaming is, he says, the mischievous sister.

"Let us beware," says he, "of allowing ourselves to give way to daydreaming, for thus we should contract the undesirable habit of allowing our attention to drowse; daydreaming is a woof on which fancy embroiders shapeless flowers, it scatters them without method or system at its own sweet will; these flowers are unreal and their colours soon fade.

"Daydreaming is a dissipation of energy, it carries us away and we cannot direct it. For this reason it is particularly dangerous, for it destroys our psychic forces and injures the development of strong mental powers."

It was with this in view, it is said, that about the twelfth century St. Dominic invented the rosary. He thought, like our Japanese philosopher, that meditation is so close akin to daydreaming that one should seek to control it by removing the temptations arising from the volatility of the imagination by means of a physical rallying of the idea.

The telling of the beads has no other object; all the decades and it a different prayer from the ten preceding it and, granting that the attention has wandered during the repetition of the ten "Hail Marys," the eleventh bead, separate from the others and appreciatively larger, comes to remind us of the change of the formula and brings back the most wandering minds to the subject of the meditation.

In short, such a director of souls as the Castilian friar knew well that daydreaming always possesses a pernicious charm, which it is well to nip in the bud.

A great thinker, nearer to our times, Condillac, says further:

"Attention is like a light which is reflected from one body onto another, in order to illuminate both of them, and I call it reflection... Sensible ideas represent to us the objects which actually impress themselves on our senses; intellectual ideas represent to us those which disappear after making their impression..."

He also says:

"Intellectual ideas, if they are familiar to us, recur to us at will." This was also the teaching of Yoritomo who writes:

"It suffices for those who practice concentration to will for the objects on which they wish to meditate to be recalled clearly before their eyes."

"Adepts in this art can, with very little effort and after placing themselves in a condition of self-absorption, transport themselves in imagination to the sphere where the phases of the occurrence which forms the subject of their thoughts unfold themselves before them."

"They will succeed in picturing to themselves places and persons in living movement, in so realistic a manner that they will even be sensible to the odours or the climate of the place that witnesses these happenings."

"What marvel that, finding themselves in this mental condition, it is easy for them to decide on sound resolutions and to thrust aside attempts to counsel for them the less studied decision?"

And he concludes:

"He who would influence others should applaud all things know how to influence himself in order to acquire the faculty of self-concentration which will allow of his reaching the highest degree of discernment."

"Many soothsayers have owed their influence over the multitude only to that spirit of concentration that passed for prophecies."

"It is wrong and delusive to give credence to magic which is trickery, but we bear within us a power equal to that of the sorcerers whose deeds are related; this is the magic of the influence which the prudent and self-possessed man always exercises over his fellows, when his intentions are pure and when his ideal is nothing else than the amelioration of the condition of others, by the wholesome influence of his example and his discourse."

# 11

## BY CONFIDENCE

Confidence is the mental impulse that all those who wish to influence others should seek to elicit. For most of them, it is the means of replacing the vacillating and ever faltering will with their own will, which they impose according to circumstances and according to the character of their followers. With some gentle persuasion is a means, even if slow, yet almost sure of success.

But we must guard the future adept from a diversity of influences, otherwise his mind will always retain the most recent impression, and before following the course of initiation we must give our attention to doing away with contradictory ideas, which he cannot completely eradicate except with great difficulty.

This is one of the characteristics of feeble folk; their stubbornness has always to be combated and we cannot succeed in teaching them confidence except after prolonged effort. The best way left to us is not to hit them too hard, for their obstinacy—which they sometimes take for willpower—would form a troublesome obstacle to their conversion. It is therefore better to seem to pay attention to their opinions, however baseless they may be, and to put before them objections that appear rather involuntary than otherwise and which to all appearances we regret the necessity of formulating.

This is what Yoritomo teaches us in the following anecdote:

"My master Lang-Ho," said he, "had among his disciples a chief who had great influence in the senate, not on account of his personal qualifications but rather of his wealth which was considerable. He had estates the extent of which gave him the privileges of a little king, and my master thought rightly that such a man should be gained over to the beauty of the Good, in order that his discourse should not be like the tares of the field but on the contrary should resemble good seed the sprouting of which brings forth a whole course of bountiful harvest."

"But this nobleman suffered from the weakness of will that hindered him from profiting by any lesson. He would say 'yes' one day and the next day, after listening to the talk of those who have no other idea except to get money out of him, he would profess an opposite opinion and set himself obstinately to follow the most pernicious counsels."

"Lang-Ho, as I have already told you, was a profound psychologist, no recess of the human heart hidden from him; so after subjecting the chief to a lengthy scrutiny, he adopted the method which seemed likely to succeed."

"He did not dissuade him from acts which under evil influences this man had made up his mind to perform, but at first he, so to speak, canalized his infatuation toward things of less importance, the plan of which he seemed at first to entertain kindly."

"He was careful thus not to awaken the spirit of obstinacy which he knew was dormant in the chief's heart. But after putting him to the test at a time when the latter was no longer in a suspicious mood, Lang-Ho enumerated to him the errors of his ways and did not fail to declare what mischief would accrue from them."

"This done, he let him follow his own devices or rather those of his evil counsellors. This policy had the result of allowing the troubles which he had foretold to arise, so that by degrees the chief began to regard Lang-Ho with a kind of superstitious fear blended with a deep veneration."

"The philosopher waited no longer; he then took in hand the freeing of his disciples from his self-interested friends, and after some months of initiation the latter, imbued with the knowledge and wisdom of the master, ceased all resistance and gloried in showing to those who depended on him that he shared the opinions of the sage."

"From that to conversion was only one step, and that step was taken so successfully that, under the influence of Lang-Ho, the chief became a genuine benefactor to all who lived on his estates and who looked up to him as a master whose word has the force of an oracle."

But certain natures are restive under persuasion or to malleable for any impression to leave its marks on them. In such, therefore, it is well to inspire confidence, somewhat in spite of themselves, by having recourse to suggestion. All modern thinkers are of this opinion; all those also who are engaged with mental infirmities:

"A suggestion of any kind being implanted in the mind," says P.E. Levy, "the organism is the better adapted to bring about realization."

We too readily give an idea of magic to the word suggestion. Suggestion, as the writer understands it, might be defined as follows: The development of competence.

It is, in a way, the imposing of one's belief on the mind of others; it is not a quack method of enthralling a person and of compelling him to carry out tasks which we feel ourselves without the courage to perform; it is a noble faculty which choice spirits alone possess, that of implanting their belief in those whom they consider worthy of being persuaded.

Be it remembered that there is suggestion in everything; in

the book which fascinates us and the theories of which gain possession of us in spite of ourselves; in the conversation to which we listen of our own accord, in the discussions of which only one side seems to us to express the truth.

But it happens too frequently that if afterward we recollect ourselves in order to judge our thoughts with the same impartiality as we should those of others, we are altogether amazed to see the fine enthusiasm that had animated us fail; the principles of the book, stripped of the magic of style, seem to us highly debatable; the conversation which we enjoyed, when the illusion of eloquence no longer illuminates it, seems to us insipid, and the object of discussion which had interested us deeply becomes a matter of indifference to us when we examine it calmly.

To what then is this sudden change to be ascribed? Does it arise from us? From our over-susceptibility to enthusiasm? From our excessive propensity to fleeting impression?

In most cases regarding these suggestions we should accuse only their authors, who, not being convinced themselves, have been unable imbue us with a lasting confidence. To inspire confidence, without which no influence is possible, several qualities are indispensable:

Sincerity with ourselves;

Hatred of injustice;

Certainty in our decisions;

Absolute truth in our predictions;

Confidence in our old merits.

Sincerity with ourselves consists especially in the conviction of the necessity which exists of making others share in a belief the effect of which we experience so deeply, that the feel cure to defuse it abroad should seem to us dereliction of all our duties.

You see why the appeal of missionaries is generally so powerful; the success of the apostolate is always subordinated to the sincerity of the convictions of him who expounds them and to his certainty that he is performing a duty in inculcating them on those for whom they may prove a support and a consolation.

If the speaker doubts his own statements, his voice will be less firm, the effulgence of his thought will less easily spread over his audience, and enthusiasm, the parent of absolute faith, will not lift them to carry he them on their way.

But how different a reception will be accorded to the apostle who is himself convinced. Let us listen to Yoritomo in this matter:

"Like a refreshing stream," said he, "the words of he who 'believes' spread into the minds of his hearers and quench their thirst of moral support and lofty convictions."

"Like moths attracted by the light of tapers, they will all flock around him who is for them the light and knows how to envelop them with its life-giving rays."

"As long as he speaks, vistas of brightness are spread before them; if he vanishes, they seem again to pass into darkness only brightened by the remembrance of the words of confidence and faith."

He who knows not hatred of injustice will never be able to exercise a salutary influence on others? How could he attract to himself confidence, the mother of conversion, if, by the unfairness of his judgements, he is subjected to that of others?

"No partiality," said Yoritomo, "should animate him who would win souls. It is by allowing himself to fall into such lapses that he will lose all authority, which he would fain acquire. Strict justice alone should direct his words and preside over his acts."

"Where he is himself quite in the dark and does not see on which side justice is ranged, he should refrain himself until the time when a close concentration permits him to see clearly before him."

"If doubt continues, let him be very careful not to a ray decision the injustice of which events might demonstrate, dust weakening the trust which his disciples are pleased to place in him. It is more honourable to confess one's ignorance that to risk committing and injustice."

To secure certainty in our judgements, it is prudent sometimes to use artifice, like the sage of whose shrewdness Yoritomo tells us:

"It should never happen," said he, "that man who wish to inspire confidence should risk seeing it destroyed by an assertion that is not borne out by facts."

"In this matter it is wise to imitate the old philosopher Hong-Yi who would never say, 'That will happen,' but, 'You have acted in such a way as to bring on yourself such or such a misfortune,' or, 'You are acting with so much prudence as to deserve to be rewarded.'"

"So that when events happened to confirm his learned forecasts, he did not fail to recall his sayings and his authority thereby increased more and more."

"It should be added that the events foreseen always came to pass, for the deducted powers Hong-Yi were great and it was easy for him to presume the acts which his disciples might be expected to perform."

But foreseeing and even prophesying are not sufficient to gain confidence and especially to communicate it. In order to implant it in the hearts of others, it is necessary to possess it—this splendid confidence in oneself that works wonders. Then it is that all those to whom thinking for themselves is a labour, those whose powers of resistance are fitful and ill-balanced, those whose moral idleness rises up against all individual initiative, will lift their heads and feel a new strength, relying on the feeling of confidence which they will experience first in the master and afterward in themselves.

The healing balm of faith will by it is good qualities impregnate them in this gentlest fashion and, despising the faint-heartedness which hitherto had marked their most trivial resolutions, they will advance fearlessly toward the goal which has become plainly visible to their sight.

It is a well-known fact that an imagined support often serves as well as the support itself. We know the instance of the child who cannot bring himself to walk without stumbling but who, as soon as we stretched out a finger to him, pretending thus to support him, steadies his steps in such a way that he can accomplish a walk of several yards without tottering.

If, however, we draw back the finger, which as it seems to them, is the support you must guard them from falling, they advance a few steps with difficulty and cannot avoid tumbling down.

It is the same with timid souls; the person who thinks he will die of fear in the solitude of an empty house will feel quite reassured if he imagines that the adjacent rooms are occupied. The presence of others, creating a feeling of confidence in possible protection, suffices to save them from the fear, which they would not fail to experience if they thought that in case of need there was no one to help them.

This protection, even when they know it to be illusory, suffices to allay their apprehensions. Thus, although they are quite sure that they can expect nothing from this intervention of a child; timid persons almost always seek such company rather than remain alone, and they experience from it a real relief.

"Every impression," says Yoritomo, "which is not our own which comes from outside is an influence which we perforce put up with. It is especially in cases of sickness that this influence can make its presence felt in the highest degree, for at such a time the subject being very week is best disposed to submit himself to any suggestion whatsoever."

"There is a vague solidarity between mind and body, which allows of the latter becoming as easy prey to others brought about by suffering. It would be idle to deny the connection between our physical ills at our mental sufferings. Some under the domination of weighty anxieties become the victims of severe headache. Others again, after repeated emotional disturbances, contract heart troubles."

"It is therefore sometimes wiser to cure the mind before considering how to care for the body, or rather it is well to effect both cures at the same time. Now it is that influence makes itself felt, triumphant, radiant; its stamps on the nerve centres an impression which reverberates through ones whole being."

"Considering that our troubles are due to pain, to anxiety, to hypochondria, we should cultivate confidence and cheerfulness which take from our conceptions their sombre colouring."

"If we have been able to inspire the invalid with competence, we shall be glad to tell him that he is getting better, for he will not doubt the truth of the assertion and that assurance will cause him to experience a real improvement."

"Then it will be in order gradually two tries that gesture on him, making clear to him the development of his cure up to the moment when he is told, 'You are cured.'"

"Miracles have no other basis them this." And the Shogun proceeds:

"But the grandest means of effecting these cures is to implant in the minds of self-imagined invalids the idea of devotion to a noble cause; to plunge them into a tide of ambition that will make them gradually forget their everlasting 'Ego.' For this over coddled 'Ego' is the real cause of most of these disorders from which all persons suffer whom a surfeit of 'Ego' so dominates that their most trivial ailments command their whole attention and seem to them to be entitled to command that of everybody else to the exclusion of all other things."

"On such influence should be exercised in quite different a manner. It will suffice to create about them an atmosphere of activity in which their personality will play a dominating part; they will us forget to spend their time in looking out for the attacks of an illness which exists only in their own brain, and he who assists them to a cure may congratulate himself doubly, for he will have made his beneficial influence felt in the case of both mind and body."

"Assuredly the best of suggestions is that which lies in, as it were, devitalizing the self-centred man, by substituting for the worshiper of his 'Ego' an altruist who, thoroughly imbued with faith in himself and strong mission with which he believes himself entrusted, will seek to impart to others the benefits of that confidence from which he has derived so much consolation."

Thus will the advice of Yoritomo be proved right when he says:

"Let him who feels himself to be in the right and has confidence in himself rise up and proclaim this faith, so that the weak, the vacillating, and all those whose suffer from doubt may flock around him to warm themselves at the genial blaze that issues from the fire of contentment of which his mindis full."

# 12

## ACQUISITION OF DOMINATING POWER

"The warriors of old," says Yoritomo, "were very fond of insignia, which they believed to be likely to impress their enemies. They liked to wear fearsome masks, the manes of beasts, or helmets the top of which represented the heads of an animal."

"One great general arrayed himself in a helmet the tip of which bore the feature of a mattock, and on the visor were engraved characters the combination of which represented the words 'mattock', 'way', and 'rock', which the learned have interpreted as follows:

"If the 'way' is not opened by my 'mattock,' I will lay it out even in the 'rock.'"

"Now what idea dominated all those warriors if not the desire to impress their enemies, some by fear, others by intimidation?"

"But there is a kind of influence a thousand-fold more valuable than all these rude methods and barbarous attempts to bring an emotion by means of bloodthirsty symbols. The domain of thought is open to all those who feel themselves unworthy of entering it; it is for those who know the turnings of a beautiful garden with multifarious paths."

"On each fresh excursion they discover psalm hitherto unknown paths which they explore always with increasing interest."

"The flowers which border them are gorgeous or poor, according as they shed on them the rays of intelligence placed at the disposal of the powers of the will which are latent in them."

"But those whose languid action cannot lift the torch, whose indolence neglects to enkindle it, do not enjoy the sight of these diversified flowers. In the gloom from which they look on them, they perceive them but indistinctly, and the path seems to them so uninteresting that they lose the desire to seek in it for new objects."

"Those, on the other hand, who know how to throw the floral beauties into the light derive from their contemplation so exquisite an enjoyment that there always arises in them the desire for fresh explorations, and also the wish to share their admiration, by introducing some persons to the marvels which they have encountered, and by teaching others how to see them in all their splendour."

"This is the secret of the dominating influence which certain man exercise over others. Those alone who know how to throw the flowers of thought into the light, after having sought and found them, can acquire sufficient power to influence the destinies of others."

This is what, in language less florid but nonetheless ornate, modern thinkers tell us:

"There is," says Durville, "an intercommunication between ourselves and others of such a nature that perpetually, night and day, we are receiving and giving fourth again influences which model us, change us, and gradually alter our mode of life."

"It is, therefore, through instigation from without that we and by making ourselves what we are: good or bad, happy or miserable."

Again Atkinson says:

"Thought plays a decisive part in human life."

"It encompasses the individual. It is the cord which binds him to his fellows and by means of which are gathered together, to join and mingle in a single current, all surrounding energies."

This is likewise the opinion of Turnbull, who recommends this method of acquiring the power necessary to first subdue those whom we wish afterward to influence:

"Lay well to heart," says he, "that this person is an instrument through which pass mental currents and that you yourself are an instrument which not only produces but also receives and retains strongly such currents to receive and retain."

"You can then begin without hesitation to make him speak, while making a judicious use of a fixed, unwavering look. Employ all your tact and finesse in doing so discreetly; at the same time you retain unmoved your own power, as if you were concentrating yourself on yourself."

"By causing mental currents to pass before your interlocutor under the form of timely questions and suggestions, you awaken in him responsive currents; you find out his likes and dislikes, and, by encouraging his confidence, through the current derived from an approval delicately expressed, you will soon succeed in making him vibrate in unison with yourself."

He who would acquire the power of domination that allows him to subdue to the action of his beneficent force the minds, which he wishes to direct, must, above all, compel himself to create between him and his disciple a client of intellectual level that will be of infinite service to him in his apostolate.

It is by creating sympathy that these vibrations in unison, so indispensable in the formation of influence, will be obtained. Sympathy begets confidence and paves the way for beneficent suggestions.

"He who knows how to attract sympathy," said Yoritomo, "is like a kindly light toward which turn all those whose minds are covered with moral darkness. Their development is rarely very speedy, and that is preferable, otherwise they would be dazzled before being enlightened; it is better to attract them slowly but irresistibly."

"Then, already imbued with the distant radiance, they will already have some out of darkness when they approach quite nearer to him who is to give them clear light and, grown familiar with the brilliant rays, they will endure its utmost intensity without flinching."

It is, in fact, one of the powers of sympathy to attract slowly but to retain surely those who feel themselves drawn to a sympathetic person by an attraction at first vague and ill defined, later justified by a thousand reasons, the principal of which, and soon the only one, will be the attraction which he possesses dominating power exerts over others.

It is better, as Yoritomo says, for this power to assert itself less roughly to have more chances of permanency. It is preferable to illumine slowly people's minds with a well-defined gleam than to dazzle them to the extent of causing them a discomfort, which will make them seek the darkness as a relief.

One of the secrets of dominating power lies in exciting similarity of feelings by adopting for the time being those that are within the compass of the person whom we wish to influence.

The feeling of condescension should be given up by strong minds; he who believes that he is lowering himself with regard to his disciple, by instilling in him principles, which he regards as too elementary, will never succeed as a director of men.

The master who would use the power of suggestion in earnest should for a moment give up his own mind to adopt the that of the man whom he is teaching; this is the only way of creating a bond of mutual confidence.

"He who would teach the first characters in writing should be able to create a child's mind in himself," said the Shogun.

We must admit that, to fulfill this condition, it is necessary to be already in possession of a rare self-mastery. Now he who can master himself is already qualified to master others.

If ambition and confidence in one's own worth are the attributes of dominating power, self-sufficiency is always the stumbling block over which he trips whom pride prevents from looking down at his feet.

Self-sufficiency almost always begets arrogance, which is of no use in producing sympathy and competence.

This exaggerated idea of "Ego" is never dictated by the consciousness of real merit, but rather by the imaginary swelling of virtues that we ascribe too freely to ourselves, as though to divert our minds with the noise of our own words.

If we wish to be sincere, we shall recognize very quickly that these virtues are imaginary, and that the parade which we make of them arises only from a great desire to possess them; that, the power having failed for assuring the gaining of them, we prefer, by proclaiming loudly that we possess them, to shirk the effort of acquiring them.

This is why self-sufficient persons, in the category of whom we must place those out of whom an empty pride beats out nobility of character, will never have the aptitude for exerting an influence over the minds of others.

Unable to derive from themselves the energy necessary to become what they would like to be, they cannot emit around themselves that power which fails them, and there domination over others will never be established.

Melancholy persons, those who are the victims of

hypochondria, are by no means destined to become shepherds of the multitude.

Melancholy almost always begets a mental condition bordering on indifference; it suppresses the desire for life, the key of all good resolutions and continual perseverance.

Every effort of the melancholy is quickly halted by that terrible, "What is the good?" which proclaims the end of everything and the vanity of life.

What influence can a man exercise whose powers of energy are destroyed by indifference and apathy? He has hardly the strength to live himself; where will he find the strength to teach others?

Cheerfulness is one of the requisite conditions for controlling others; not that boisterous mirth which is made up of bursts of laughter, the reasons for which are not always of the most refined nature, but that inward peace which we define as cheerfulness and which is the mark of highly developed minds.

A man of fine character will never be melancholy; hypochondria is the trademark of the incapable; it is the commencement of manias and of all crazes that desolate humanity and abase its moral level.

The philosophers of ill omen whose teaching has clouded so many young brains have defined enjoyment as follows:

Ah, well! But is not that worth an effort, to suffer no longer, and can we regard as a madman the man who labourers to end this suffering, by substituting for it the joy of living, which opens men's minds to the cult of beauty?

The art of happiness lies especially in the great wish to live. If Yoritomo was not willing to raise the burning question of free will, he nonetheless admits the unquestionable influence of each one of us on our own destiny.

"Men," said he, "are for the most part like the fool who

shivered, cowering in a snowdrift, while around him the sun bathed the mountain with its burning rays. He cursed the snow, the cold, the hateful country where he dwelled, and the misery of his existence which had to be spent in suffering and barrenness."

"In vain people signaled to him of nearby paths, in vain for they showed him from afar flowers gathered on the way; he was obstinately bent on doing nothing to free himself from his sufferings and continued to curse the place which it would have been so easy to leave and deplored the unhappiness of the fate which had caused him to be born in that inclement country."

Have we not here in very truth the picture of the pessimist who denies the existence of happiness and beauty while pretending to turn away when they pass his door?

Such persons may perchance exercise a pernicious influence over weak minds, but it will always be limited, for—we cannot repeat it too often—real influence over others is only acquired at the price of complete mastery of oneself.

This mastery should be the aim of the efforts of the man who wishes to possess this faculty and to make use of it for his own happiness and that of those with whom he comes in contact.

"Again," said the Nippon philosopher, "we should keep ourselves from too commonplace associations, for, granting this truth that the thought which we emit about us is taken in by those around, we ought to beware of the imbibing of commonplace thought which, when repeat too often, will end by occupying, unknown to ourselves, a place in our brain and will weaken the quality of the power."

"The higher type of man should never harbor a medley of ideas. He who frames thoughts the waves of which spread themselves around him succeeds, by a succession of adulatory movements which may be compared with those of sound, in striking the intelligence of others by setting their brains in vibration, in other words, in a state to receive the floating thought."

"But the really forceful man, one whose secret energies are concentrated on the gaining of influence, one whose aim is to acquire dominating power, will harbor no ignoble thoughts, for he will not barter away the first to arrive of these flowers of the mind; if he finds himself among people of small intellectual caliber he will surpass them with all the mighty power that his knowledge and his strength of will confer on him."

"He will know how to listen to them, then to talk to them, perhaps to convince them, but not for a moment will he submit himself to imbibing their commonplace thoughts, for having come among them in the spirit of an apostle he is too conscious of his own excellence, he knows too well his own superiority, he is, in a word, on too lofty a pedestal to allow himself to be affected by things beneath him."

"Does the granite stoop to the ivy that twines itself about it while mounting toward the towers in its need of protection and support?"

The Shogun remarks also that this plant, which without the support of the granite, would trail miserably off the ground, ends, when it has covered the surface at every point by forming an essential part of the building, to such a degree that its frail tendrils effect more for the durability of the works of man then the hardest marbles chiseled by the most skillful workmen. And he asked:

"How many ancient towers, that seemed of unquestionable solidity, crumble to pieces when deprived of the parasites that seemed to overrun them?"

"So it is with all those who possess power; they maintain themselves only because they create disciples whose devotion serves to consolidate their work. But if they cannot retain the influence which a first they have sent forth around them, their followers fall away one by one, and the man left alone soon sees the edifice of his superiority crumbled to pieces."

"Dominating power," Yoritomo proceeds, "is developed especially by an apostolate the exercise of which, by creating a mental current between the master and those whom he is teaching, wards off opposing currents."

In the cant of modern science it is said in fact that material builders, drawn by the attractive force of thought, are always displeased in feeble minds by a stronger influence, but that the converse does not hold good.

Such is the comment of the Japanese philosopher when he tells us:

"Do not rub shoulders with a commonplace mind except with intention of raising him to your own level, but do not think of entering into mental communion with such before making it worthy of it."

This luminous sentence may serve as a commentary on Yoritomo's entire teaching, for every line of his writings is an appeal to energy, an invitation to the practice of the cult of moral beauty, and an encouragement to that advance toward the Better, which should guide our steps toward the enchanted temple on the facade of which are emblazoned these eternal words: Truth, Coverage, and Cheerfulness.